Words, whether

spoken or read
heard or written,
trigger

images in the mind, and these
images come from

metaphor or experiences.

Sentences have a

3 part structure   separate from the words embedded in them.

grammatical   expectation   rhetorical   spoken/written   images
correctness   efficiency   effectiveness

metaphor   experiences

Paragraphs

Contract   Sentences

Character Concept Significance   Structure   Words

Gram – Expect – Rhetoric   sp/wrt – images

Old – new

Signif or Insignif   Met   exp

Four verbal arts related to words:

listening speaking reading writing

Writing and Research for College

The Structures of Imaginative Literacy

Second Edition

Bill Koch

University of Northern Iowa

Cover image © Shutterstock, Inc.

Kendall Hunt
publishing company

www.kendallhunt.com
Send all inquiries to:
4050 Westmark Drive
Dubuque, IA 52004-1840

Copyright © 2010, 2014 by Kendall Hunt Publishing Company

Text ISBN: 978-1-5249-5412-3
PAK ISBN: 978-1-5249-5413-0

Published in the United States of America

Contents

# Epigrams

When social crises seem immune to solutions offered by present understanding, it is then that Life may be expected to seek out a new order of reality, a new understanding, as a pattern superimposed upon intelligence. Eventually, intelligence will depend on this new primary organization, this new paradigm.
George Towner
The Architecture of Knowledge (1980)

At the rate of progress since 1800, every American who lived into the year 2000 would know how to control unlimited power. He would think in complexities unimaginable to an earlier mind. He would deal with problems altogether beyond the range of earlier society.
Henry Adams
The Education of Henry Adams (1904)

After having been completely occupied in constructing organisms, the developments [in biology] to be expected are primarily of the intellectual and moral order. Life is only now beginning to develop its internal dispositions, concentrating its attention and care on advances and refinements of a finally perfected consciousness.
Pierre Teilhard de Chardin
Writings in Time of War (1917)

You have only to work up imagination to the state of vision, and the thing is done.
William Blake
(in Gilchrist's *The Life of William Blake*)

If a student can—and this is most difficult and unusual—draw back, get a critical distance on what he clings to, come to doubt the ultimate value of what he loves, he has taken the first and most difficult step toward the philosophic conversion.
Allan Bloom
The Closing of the American Mind (1987)

Education will be saved only when it is agreed that men should know the same things— which does not mean that they believe the same things. It means that they will be protected, in the only way education can bring this about, against mass judgments at the eleventh hour.
Mark Van Doren
Liberal Education (1943)

Introduction

Imagination is not to be divorced from facts: it is a way of illuminating the facts. It enables students to construct an intellectual vision of a new world, and it preserves the zest of life by the suggestion of satisfying purpose.

—From Alfred North Whitehead, *Aims of Education*, p. 93

The first edition of this textbook had the subtitle, "Developing an Imaginative Literacy," but over the past three years that I've used this textbook, I've identified some ideas that I think are enduring (at least for the foreseeable future) and so I'm testing them out as "structures" of imaginative literacy, structures to be polished as much as possible, adjusted to meet any exigency.

Among the ideas that I've discovered during the past three years as enduring are the following:

1. The college student needs to be aware of two readerships when in college: civilian and academic.

2. College education is adult education, whether one remains in academics or goes back to civilian life. But college gives students a college-level engagement with words (a CLEW) that you need whether you are an academic or a civilian.

3. There are verbal activities going on automatically in the human mind, and the adult with a CLEW seizes control of those verbal activities and uses them deliberately.

4. Once students have a CLEW, their thinking becomes visceral as well as cerebral.

5. College is considered the place where students encounter radical and revolutionary ideas, but what is really radical and revolutionary is that students have these experiences by examining things that they are most familiar with—like words.

6. Students need to scrub some ideas off the body of understanding that they bring into college.

7. They need to detach their beliefs from their understanding of those beliefs and transform their understanding, pivoting from a childhood-level understanding to an adult-level understanding.

These insights reinforce even more the statement by Wayne C. Booth and Marshall W. Gregory in the Preface to their textbook on rhetoric (*The Harper and Row Rhetoric: Writing as Thinking; Thinking as Writing*): "We have long been convinced that the required first-year writing course can provide the most important of all college experiences."

After several years of teaching the first-year writing course at the University of Northern Iowa, I hardly agree with their claim. During this time, I've used different handbooks (but not the Booth and Gregory one!), and as writing teachers already know, most of these textbooks are very similar in content. As for the students taking this course, many teachers have mentioned that the students seemed unengaged with writing and reading, and often left the course—what should be the most important of all courses—unengaged with language.

This book tries to do something about this lack of engagement, and to show why first-year writing courses are such an important experience for students, I try to get them to have this more personal engagement with words before they apply words to any specific writing assignment that they are given. Even more, I think that their reading experiences will be more profitable after they examine the phenomena of words and their own understanding of verbal phenomena. It has been my experience that when students examine their understanding of and engagement with words, and see that this course deals with only two modes of verbal phenomena (the literacy modes), they then are ready to engage their minds with verbal texts at a level (or depth) that college teachers will be pleased with.

Special Features

- As you have likely noticed, this book features an unusual entity on the inside front cover and on the back, which I've called "**Wedges of Knowledge**." These things arose from my interaction with Mark Van Doren's claim that we like the person whose distinctions refresh and liberate us. It occurred to me that we can create distinctions that contrast understandings of concepts (like realism) and that also differentiate aspects of a single concept (like human consciousness).

- Prominent in most chapters are **lists of various kinds and lengths**. Also prominent is the attempt to **use popular movies and current events** to motivate students to be critical of their own assumptions and viewpoints.

- Several essays are reprinted here, one of which helps students develop the right assumptions about their engagement with words. The other essays challenge the students with provocative theses, but the students also examine the essays for the writers' style of writing.

- I've included some activities that I created during the past six years as I've pursued my own refresher course in composition theory. Two of these activities I've called **Letter Linkage** and **Flush-Left Diagramming** (FLD). As I've explored the implications of FLD, I've developed other concepts to help students see the structures of verbal texts beyond the words embedded in those texts.

- These concepts will help students develop critical thinking skills related to their reading skills as well as help them with the revision stages of their writing assignments.

- Tear-Out Sheets (TOS) have been incorporated so that there is consistency of instruction across the course.

- Most ambitiously, this book attempts to identify verbal and critical thinking competencies that the student will then see as structures of consciousness and inherent to adult-level thinking and communication in whatever environment that person is in.

Emphasis On

- Personal engagement with words
- The metaphorical dimension of words
- Getting critical distance on verbal articulations
- The aspect of "perfection" in the process of a writing or reading assignment: we can speak of a level of perfection proper to each stage
- The way revision produces our best insights, which then get into the final draft
- How reading becomes more powerful and fruitful when the reader's mind is sensitive to the metaphorical dimension in the texts he or she is reading

What this Text Does Not Have

- No exhaustive list of possible sources and their bibliographies
- No assignments for the various genres of writing emphasized in college
- Nothing much of what is already found in most college writing handbooks

Rationale

Because a college education is so expensive these days, I hope that this book does nothing short of giving students ways to have a transformation of consciousness, and in such a way that they know that they have had an experience of transformation (which, in reality, is priceless). We never seem to explain very well what behaviors would signal that a student has had a transformative experience or is transformed. It also seems that we always come up short of our envisagement of what we believe a transformative experience feels like as well as looks like.

I think we assume a transformed consciousness would not have problems, or would solve problems more easily, or would always make us happy and patient. Well, I think we can learn to be patient, although we will have times of sorrow and frustration. And we will continue to have challenges and problems, and sometimes we won't be able to solve some problems. But at least we will still know that our college education not only equipped us with tools for our jobs but for our humanity.

So, the students will experience challenges of the first order in this course, the kind that can change them radically. But let me clarify what it means to have a transformation of consciousness: it means that you have awakened your imagination.

Imagination

I know that seems too simple of a clarification, but it has been my experience that when I examine the word–image dynamic that I explain in the book, something linked to the intellect is "awakened." This is the imagination. When I see how words trigger images in my mind, and how those images might be too simplistic for the reality that the words are pointing too, I awaken to a new experience of the imagination – and of my intellect. Indeed, I then see more clearly how the imagination is connected to metaphor, as metaphors trigger specific images in the mind.

Speaking of metaphors, maybe instead of saying that college wakes up the imagination, I should say college liberates the imagination from the mental prison it is in when students enter college. College liberates the imagination from the prison of unexamined assumptions that students bring into college. As students examine and change the assumptions about words and thinking that they bring into college, they release their imagination from the prison of automatic verbal activities. When students seize control of these automatic verbal activities, the imagination then helps them identify—and test—better ways and better words to describe their experiences. They break into a new field of freedom, an unexpected field, but natural enough to life's self-conscious element.

Expectations

Perhaps I can reword this last point: As students examine the assumptions they bring into college about words and education and history, they scrub ideas off the structure of understanding that they brought into college. They scrub these ideas off as they practice at a deeper level some of the verbal activities they've been using since they were children. They are then doing what Whitehead notes in the quotation that started this Introduction: They clarify their understanding of the purposes of life that they had been taught in childhood, and they can see more clearly the intellectual vision of a new world that they'd also been taught in childhood. I like to use the following figures to illustrate my point:

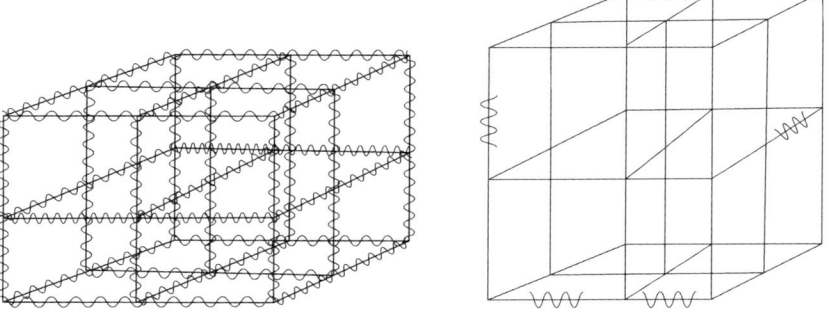

Structure of understanding brought into college with ideas deeding scrubbed off if adult wants adult level thought process: childlike and unbiased receptivity

The lesson here is that students necessarily come into college with ideas about words and the educational experience and their understanding that should likely not be on their body of understanding when they leave college, or when they finish the general education portion of college—or this course on writing at the college level. But of course, students can choose not to examine these ideas, and so for such students their reception of ideas in college or after college is never as clear as it could be. Such students filter the views of others through the lenses of inadequate adult understanding, but they assume that the problem resides in the views that are being presented to them. Perhaps those views do have their errors. But the adults don't have that unbiased receptivity that the cube on the right in the illustration represents, and so they cannot be sure that they are producing quality critical thinking judgments about the merits of their wording in essays or other writing assignments, nor about the merits of someone else's arguments.

Transformation

It turns out, then, that transformation is not the vague term that we have been left with when it has been explained to us in the past. Now we have a concrete abstraction to link to it—reader expectations and the word–image dynamic. Both of those activities activate the imagination—no, that is too vague: **Both of those activities illuminate aspects of student thinking that had escaped their attention.**

The transformation of consciousness begins with an intellectual perception of the connection between words and imagination, and yet the imagination then releases into consciousness some intellectual energy that clarifies our understanding of and engagement with words; and scholars speculate that words—spoken words—bounced human consciousness out of a purely instinctual consciousness, an instinctual consciousness that had experienced rich symbolic activity in the brain, but with no tool to give meaning to the activity.

And students wonder why they have to take writing and speech courses in college!

But when we understand our historical context with the accuracy and precision of scientific analysis, we should expect to experience this kind of consciousness phenomena.

It is time for this kind of intellectual experience.

It is time college gave students their money's worth—and that it fulfill its own destiny.

Features of The Second Edition

I've envisioned this book as a kind of primer for the college student entering college, and so I envision it as a text that would be helpful in those first-year programs that go by various names, such as Cornerstone. It is with that intention in mind that the first chapter asks (challenges?) students to examine the assumptions that they bring into college, because more than likely faculty have different views about those assumptions. The first chapter focuses on assumptions that students have about words and writing, but it also treats other assumptions that affect how students approach all their classes in college.

This second edition's layout is completely different from that of the first edition. For example, I've taken one of my activities called flush-left diagramming (FLD) and expanded the three-page coverage in the first edition into its own long and detailed chapter. I've focused on the features of sentence structure because the sentence is the smallest verbal unit by which we get an idea across to others. If students are not very cogent about the features of the sentence—especially with regard to reader expectations—then their revision of paragraphs, as well as other revisions, will be ineffectual.

Another unique chapter is the one on the Principles of Reader Expectations (PRE). This list of expectations is an adaptation of the "principles of writing clearly" that Joe

Williams articulated in his book *Style: The Basics of Clarity and Grace*. In that brilliant book, he often mentioned that the writer can identify those sentences that the reader would wish the writer had revised, and so it occurred to me that I could change his list into "reader expectations." I can't emphasize enough the debt I owe to Dr. Williams and his book. As it turns out, he identified "expectations" that are working below the consciousness of most readers. These expectations are not those of grammar or of rhetoric but those dealing with the relationships of subjects to their verbs and such. By naming those expectations, we have not only a good revision tool but also a good reading (and rereading) tool.

I also emphasize the reading of words as much as the writing of words in this text, even though I don't formally treat reading until Chapter 4. Still, it is obvious that students do more formal reading in the first weeks of college before they do any formal and extended writing, and it is for that reason that Chapter 2 is about the phenomena of words, whether read or heard. This chapter continues to be interesting because of the reality of images being triggered in our minds by words, whether we read the words or hear them.

Perhaps the most problematic part of this textbook is the research project chapter. I outline a specific topic for research rather than offer generic explanations of what constitutes college-level research. I am not deprecating college-level research, but I am distinguishing academic research from college-level research, equating college education with adult education, and emphasizing for adult education the focus that Northrop Frye felt is the one proper to the university: "It might be better," he wrote in 1969, "if the university confined itself to supplying the historical dimension of its culture."

With that in mind, I ask students to read up on what scholars say seems to be the history of the formation of texts (and people) that cultures have called sacred or inspired. This means in most cases that students will be reading the work of scholars who examine texts that they had been told in childhood were very necessary (or, for that matter, not necessary) for good adult living. In either case, it is likely that students will come into college with a level of understanding that isn't at the adult level, but that is (for all intents and purposes) at the childhood level. I feel that the skeptics of religion are as much CLEW-less as the defenders of religion. All need to be shaken up. All students bring into college ideas about these texts and about religion (and science) in general that need to be examined and likely scrubbed off their structure of understanding if they want to be admitted into the realm of adult-level thinking. In integrating a historical perspective into their understanding, students aren't so much changing their beliefs as changing their understanding of them from a childhood level to an adulthood level. That other ramifications manifest themselves in the process really only shows that students are having a radical experience, one that gets to the "roots" of things. Welcome to college—to adult education.

Another new feature of this edition is a chapter called "Proto-Essays." Here I've offered three essays on topics that I think all college students should treat during their time in college, in adult education. I only provide several paragraphs of each essay, and follow them with questions that prompt the student to complete a draft of the essay. In doing this, students get a sense of what they can achieve as ordinary adult thinkers and writers with a "CLEW."

The penultimate chapter attempts to mirror the first chapter by offering a survey of our historical situation. This chapter began the first edition but students didn't understand why I discussed many non-literacy topics in a book on writing. When I assigned the chapter at the end of the semester, its purpose was more obvious. We truly do live in historic times and our assets and liabilities can be perceived—I believe—with unprecedented clarity because we have this imaginative literacy.

Of course, the student and reader of the textbook is welcome to read any chapters at any time, but this order seems to mirror the intellectual journey of first-year students.

Tear-Out Sheets—and a Plea

In order to keep everyone on the "same page," this book has many pages that are to be torn out and handed in as assignments. Because of this, students can't sell the book back, but it is hoped that they will find the book helpful enough to keep it as a resource. The testimony of one such student is on the back cover of the textbook, and I hope that many others will share her sentiments. In any case, it is hoped students will resist the temptation to resale a book that is gutted and so not helpful to incoming students.

CHAPTER 1

Examining Assumptions Brought into College

There can be no sense of excitement or discovery, no glimpsing of new worlds of the mind, without [the teacher] dramatizing for the student the mental attitude that is inductive and empirical, putting the learner in the same psychological position as the most original of thinkers.
(Northrop Frye, *The Stubborn Structure*, 99)

Goals:

- Be aware of differences in student and faculty assumptions.
- Integrate faculty assumptions into student body of assumptions.
- Understand the developmental nature of the maturation of assumptions in the student.
- Understand the basic elements of liberal education.

Outcomes:

- Explain the purposes of liberal education.
- Articulate how faculty assumptions complement or complete the assumptions students bring into college.
- Begin to word explanations more accurately and precisely.

Terms to Know:

- Three consciousnesses of liberal education
- Three traits of a liberated consciousness
- Cognitive dissonance
- Childhood-level understanding
- Adulthood-level understanding
- Inadequate adult understanding
- Enlightened adult understanding

It has been my experience that when students enter the college classroom, they bring with them a set of assumptions and attitudes about language and education that are often at odds with those that the teacher brings into the classroom. When the students and teacher are not on the same page in this regard, a lot of misunderstanding occurs from the first hour onward. To preclude that possibility, at the beginning of a new course I like to list what I think are assumptions and attitudes that students bring into the classroom. My aim isn't to make them—as a student described it one semester—throw out everything they've learned so far. It is only to give them some ideas to add to what they already know or assume—although they often see that some ideas they have been using likely need to be scrubbed off their body of assumptions. Students tend to begin college with the following assumptions. ◎

Assumptions Students Bring into College

1. They need a bigger vocabulary to write at the college or adult level.
2. They must have a thought before they start writing.
3. They can't make mistakes in their answers, even (or especially) in their first attempts.
4. Words are used only to convey what they already know.
5. The arts are superfluous to developing what's important for being successful at a job or in a career.
6. Critical thinking is a matter of finding flaws in someone's argument or opinion.

7. A college education is a matter of gathering more information, but the information doesn't affect their level of understanding things.

8. College forces them to change the beliefs that they were taught in childhood.

9. College's reputation for making students radical and revolutionary is not to be admired or applied to many students.

Faculty come into the classroom with the following assumptions that tend to **augment** the student assumptions just listed.

Faculty Assumptions

1. A bigger vocabulary isn't necessarily going to produce college-level writing, but a better use of the words already on the page will likely do the trick.

2. Although it would be nice to have thoughts before you start to write, thinking is done with words, so just write, and then thinking will occur, and thoughts will flood your mind.

3. The college approach to writing as a process allows for error and messiness in the early stages, then it gives students the tools to convert the messy and the mistaken into organized and accurate answers.

4. Words do convey what students know, but that is only half of it: students can examine their words in ways that produce real knowledge, and this knowledge can be as foundational as the learning produced by science.

5. The arts are a language that students should practice as much as they practice science, although the emphasis should first be on practicing subskills perfectly, *not* on presenting a perfect final product. Then students see that there is an artistic dimension to their success in any task—there is an artistic element in their most ordinary prose!

6. Critical thinking in students is more than finding flaws; it is also finding common ground hidden from the eyes of their present body of assumptions. This means they examine their own assumptions as well as those of others.

7. A liberal education can do more than give students information; it can liberate them from unconscious habits of thinking and expression, and release in them powers of critical thinking that produce liberating and refreshing distinctions.

8. College asks students to distinguish their beliefs from their *understanding* of their beliefs. When they make that distinction, they realize that they come into college with a depth of understanding that is at the childhood level. Such an understanding cannot really produce enlightened, adult-level understanding. Students can achieve adult-level understanding of the things they were taught in childhood and still retain their allegiance to those things.

9. Faculty try to show that college courses are only asking students to think at the adult level, and what makes this level of thinking and understanding revolutionary and radical is that it occurs because students see new aspects of things that you they been familiar with their entire lives—like words (especially words!).

What is Liberated in Liberal Education?

We should spend some time thinking about what the word *liberal* means in the term *liberal education*. It is not meant in the political sense—as if college is to make everyone vote Democratic—but in the historical sense. In its traditional sense, *liberal* means a nobility of spirit or having largeness of heart. That is not a bad thing to have. But we should also see liberal education in the context of education in the West. Liberal education—or college education, according to Mark Van Doren—can be seen as the second of the two stages of education that adults in the modern world need. The first stage comprises both grade school and high school education and is referred to simply as "elementary" in Van Doren's book *Liberal Education*.

This basic distinction isn't as unjust as it might sound at first. In the early part of the 20th century, John Dewey asked—is education a function of society or is society a function of education? We can answer his either/or question by using Van Doren's two stages of education. One could then say that education is a function of society when students are going through K–12. This education teaches the student—as Frye mentions in the essay you will read—the basic skills to be a competent citizen of the state. Due to this, it is necessarily one sided, and what society needs. But, when the students get to liberal education (LE), they have to take a critical stance on the intellectual matrix that they bring into college, the understanding of things that was formed in their K–12 schooling, as Allan Bloom alludes to in the statement in the Epigrams of this textbook. They then see that the understanding they brought into college is naturally not at the adult level, and college helps them to achieve adult-level understanding.

Of course, as students improve their understanding, they also understand how society—adults who are at the helms of society's institutions—might still be using an inadequate adult understanding. So the students sharpen the critical thinking skills that are needed to improve society: they become (to use another phrase from Van Doren) citizens of the republic of human understanding.

It turns out, then, that college exists to make **society a function of education**—as bizarre as this might sound to students just entering college. That is, college-educated students will graduate from college and enter the workforce and the other institutions of modern society (institutions like government, science, religion, media) and restructure any aspects in those institutions that are not nurturing the humane values that college had inculcated in them during the Liberal Arts Core (LAC) portion of their college education.

What follows are diagrams that outline the outcomes of the LAC (also called *general education*). These outcomes will not likely impact you now in your first weeks of college, but as you experience the rest of the LAC (or general education) and then courses in your major, you will likely see that these terms organize the diversity or the universe of experiences that your college gives you.

It seems to me, after being involved with LE in some way for the past 40 years, and being involved with our society's economic structures off and on during that time, that students can develop three consciousnesses or perspectives while in college, as shown in the accompanying figure.

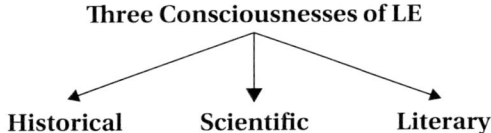

Three Consciousnesses of LE

Historical   **Scientific**   **Literary**

The names that I give for these perspectives are pretty common, but I would submit that students coming into college often have an inadequate understanding of history and science, and often have no understanding of literary consciousness. Again, I would not expect students to have such a high level of differentiated awareness until after they have submitted to the disciplines of LE. But after students go through the LAC, they should have something like a historical consciousness that sees how the past is informing the present, and what is unique to the present that didn't exist until now. **They should also have the ability to word their explanations more accurately and precisely than ever before**, and so achieve one of the main intellectual goals of science. And as for the literary, they should now have an enlightened adult understanding of the "story" of their lives within the larger narrative of nation and religion that they were taught in childhood. And their historical consciousness will help them see that for all the epochal breakthroughs they are witnessing or helping to produce, they are only being responsible with their intellect in ways that adults in earlier eras were responsible, and that the adults of those eras would applaud our responsible use of our intellectual heritage and tools.

In the meantime, way before they enter this literary consciousness, they will already be experiencing what I call the three traits of a liberated consciousness, as shown in the accompanying figure.

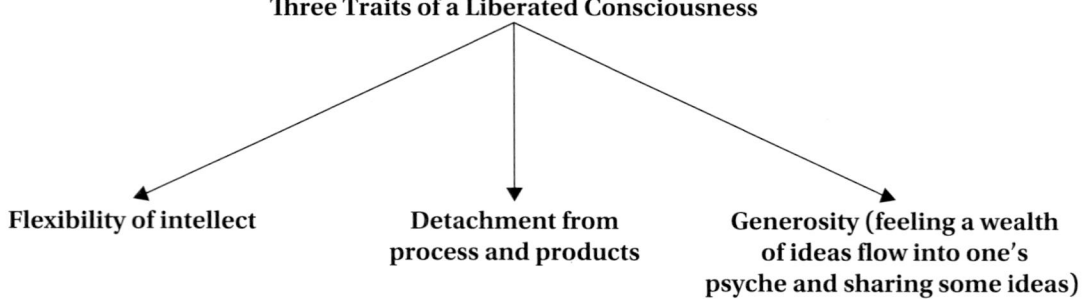

Three Traits of a Liberated Consciousness

Flexibility of intellect   **Detachment from process and products**   **Generosity (feeling a wealth of ideas flow into one's psyche and sharing some ideas)**

Flexibility of the intellect refers to students' ability to produce verbal artifacts that are able to reach the intended audience, whereas detachment from process and product means that they are free of the need for most forms of external validation. The achievement of these two intellectual goals then seems to burst a psychical flood gate, and students feel a wealth of ideas flooding their intellect and making it easier for them to produce high-quality verbal artifacts.

College faculty, then, want students to construct an intellectual matrix that is *not* a one-sided vision and understanding of things and of thinking. Faculty help students see that some ideas need to be scrubbed off the structure of understanding that they bring into college. College doesn't force students to remove anything they don't want to remove. But the intellectual exercises that college asks students to submit to improve their intellectual muscles, and the students themselves see the cogency of scrubbing off some ideas that, were they to remain on the student body of assumptions, would only produce inadequate adult understanding. In addition, the faculty are not saying that all the learning that the students had brought into college is wrong, but they do want to make students face the possibility that their understanding is one sided, incomplete, or underdeveloped.

As
they analyze
        the understanding of things that
they brought
        into college,
students might see
        that
they have
        to jettison some ideas that

they'd garnered
　　　　in childhood, and
they might resist
　　　　doing this.
They might also feel
　　　　that
they are being forced
　　　　to jettison such ideas.
　　　　However,
college would not be forcing
　　　　them to abandon anything
they are loathe
　　　　to abandon.

Still, faculty have been through this furnace of self-examination and have to vary-ing degrees attained those traits of the liberated intellect. In addition, they know that many adults in the outside world never underwent this self-examination, and every indication is that these adults continue to use—all throughout their adult years—their childhood-level understanding (which makes for inadequate adult understanding). It could very well be that the social crises that Towner says seem immune to present-day solutions could be solved if adults would recognize that they are using childhood-level understanding during their adult years. Not to be harsh in my indictment, but we should say that their thinking is childish, not childlike: Were it "childlike," they would be willing to superimpose on their intelligence a new pattern of reality, test it out, and live with the results.

The following diagram tries to capture in images this adult intellectual challenge:

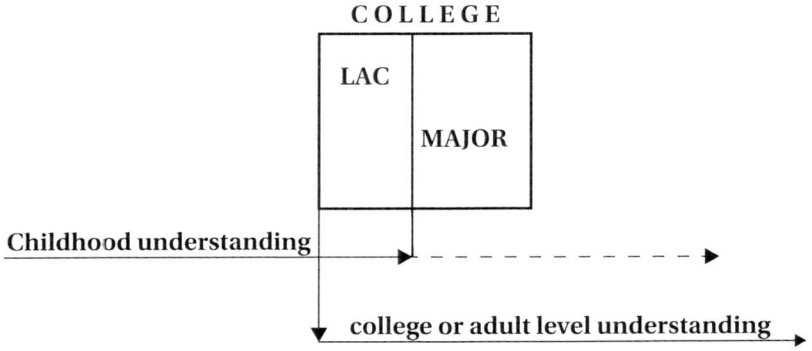

Notice that the understanding of things resulting from K–12 education is used in the first part of college. This is natural, as the student cannot help but bring into college the level of understanding he or she attained in childhood. And college-level understanding builds on this level, although it requires students to examine the body of assumptions that they bring into college. This is where the "battle" or mental fight comes in, and—unfortunately—it can be avoided by the student. The broken line that extends "Childhood understanding" beyond the LAC portion of college and then parallels "College- or adult-level understanding" represents the reality that many adults use childhood-level understanding for their entire lives.

Critical Distancing and Cognitive Dissonance

The Epigrams contain a statement by Allan Bloom that is relevant here. He claims that college asks students to undergo a philosophic conversion, and this entails getting a critical distance on the things they cling to and recognizing that they do not possess (yet) an ultimate understanding of the things they love.

This critical distancing causes cognitive dissonance: an anxious feeling resulting from the conflict between two seemingly logical claims or conclusions. The most intense anxiety arises when students are examining those things that they were taught in childhood as being essential to their happiness. These things are rooted in two areas: popular culture and religion. Popular culture tells students that they need the objects of commerce in order to have a full life and to be popular. Their religious instruction likely has told them that certain narratives must be adhered to if they are to achieve eternal happiness. But if students can examine these things with the critical distance that comes with a deeper level of understanding, they will examine the values that society espouses as central to human happiness. They will notice that they have accepted these values without criticism, and they will now be concerned that this society seems pretty chaotic as they look at the headlines in the newspaper—ah, when they look online, on the "Web."

When it comes to religious issues, I think it is very important for students to realize that they can and should distinguish the belief or narrative from their understanding of that belief or value. They bring into college a childhood-level understanding of that narrative or belief. They must admit that they do not have the ultimate or even an adult understanding of that narrative or belief, and college can help them get closer to having an adult-level understanding.

Another issue might be more prominent first: that is, the upcoming dissonance between the modern call for "openness to alternative views" and the demands of critical thinking. Most students assume that besides giving them skills for a job, college will develop their critical thinking skills. But critical thinking involves coming to conclusions on issues and sometimes determining that some claims are just in error, or mistaken, or out of bounds. Such judgments can be interpreted as a lack of openness. This is an issue that remains a festering boil on the academic body.

Resolution and Flowering into the Enlightened Stage

A tug-of-war goes on in students' minds as they grapple with the new information and its challenges to the understanding that they brought into college—they learn information that directly confronts their current understanding. They are challenged by the contrary calls of being open and thinking critically. This mental fight is illustrated by the crisscross of lines in the following diagram:

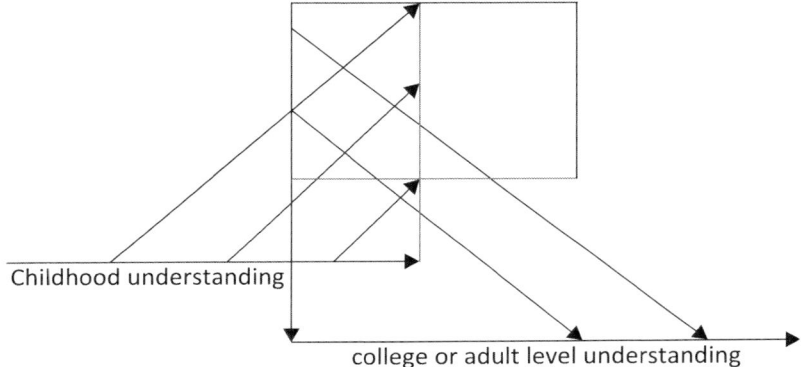

Childhood understanding

college or adult level understanding

I think it is important to understand that this mental battle—and victory—should occur during the LAC portion of college. It is during this part of a college education when students examine the understanding of things that they brought into college and determine how to improve their understanding of those values and concepts so that the ideas learned in childhood continue to have relevance and cogency during the decades following their graduation. This conversion must take place while in the LAC portion of college, because students' major courses merely train them for a job in the economic system of modern society. The major course of study is not meant to not call into question the humaneness of that economic system, or how its present configuration can be sustained in the light of social and economic realities.

The "Body" of Assumptions Acquired through Liberal Education

Students can imagine themselves as Jake Sully in the movie *Avatar*. Jake tried out a new body (of assumptions) and found that the larger frame of mind (represented by the Na'vi physical body) fit his growing awareness of who he was. But in his experiences of getting used to that body, disciplining himself in mind and body, he had to engage in warfare with his old self, represented by the economic forces and their mercenary security interests. But as students become more intimately engaged with their words, they learn that words are the mightiest swords, and they will use them to conquer their old matrix for understanding things. In this process, they will attain a more structured, "larger" brain, a brain that has an inner richness that matches the external richness of the commercial civilization that they were born into, a civilization that has been around for just 6,000 years.

So I like to think that in awakening the imagination, in integrating the assumptions of liberal education, students "wake up" with their personalities intact, like Jake did at the end of *Avatar*, but in a larger body of assumptions and with an array of intellectual resources that help them engage fruitfully now, while in college, with challenges that come from beyond the college campus. These challenges, they will see, come mostly from the economic realm, and those challenges will likely be the center of their attention after they leave college. But with their newly achieved, correct perspective on economics (a measured, proportionate perspective, imaginative and realistic), they will likely be agents of productive change in this aspect of their new lives.

Fools act on imagination
without knowledge;
pedants act on knowledge
without imagination.
The task of the university
is to weld together
imagination and experience.

Alfred North Whitehead

CHAPTER 2

The Phenomena of Words in the Light of Enlightened Adult Understanding

"The soul," says Aristotle, "never thinks without images," and it is among images that distinctions are found. (Mark Van Doren, *Liberal Education* 126)

The thinner metaphors of animal and machine ...are seldom recognized as functions of our speech. (Mark Van Doren, *Liberal Education* 21)

Goals:

- Become more deeply engaged with the language brought into college.

Outcomes:

- Demonstrate a sensitivity and be able to describe to the images triggered in the adult mind by words learned in childhood.
- Demonstrate an awareness of the mind's automatic use of metaphors to explain facts, and seize control of this automatic use of metaphors.

Terms to Know:

- Physical literalism
- Metaphorical literalism
- Letter Linkage

Introduction

In the prior chapter, I mentioned that college should be viewed as adult education, at least the Liberal Arts Core (LAC) or general education part of college. The content of the LAC should be the same for all students, no matter what their major; it should expose students to the history of their past and to the achievements and failures of their ancestors. The LAC should also give students the ability to think more critically about the key issues of their day and to formulate arguments that merit serious consideration by others.

The gist is that students will recognize that they come into college with a level of understanding that is in many key ways still a childhood-level understanding, and they must now do some intellectual work to get an adult-level understanding. But this adult-level understanding isn't achieved just by adding more information to the warehouses of information students bring into college. Something else is required; it is like a changing of worlds. But that rather nebulous description can be made more concrete when students consider two things that occur automatically in the human mind: (1) words trigger images in the adult mind and (2) the mind automatically uses metaphors to describe facts and experiences. Students can then examine the images triggered in their minds by words they learned in childhood. These words need not be overt metaphors, and may simply be key words carried along from childhood. But when students begin using metaphors deliberately, they then harness the intellectual energies that those images represent. Students then realize that they are revising their understanding of beliefs that they'd been taught in childhood, and now they understand how those beliefs can help them direct those harness intellectual energies so these energies help solve specific problems that adults in the modern world face.

The exercises in this chapter will help you, as students in the LAC, seize control of that which goes on automatically in the human mind. In the process, you will also begin to scrub off some ideas that you brought into college on your body of assumptions. This chapter's activities will help you examine the images triggered by words, whether those words are overt metaphors or not, and help you explore the images and entailments related to words that are used as metaphors. The result will be twofold: (1) you will have a better understanding of the topics for which you've used specific words and (2) you will have a better understanding of the role of words in your life.

Letter linkage

Stirring Up Words in Your Mind

A limber mind is necessary for examining the topics in this chapter, and thus the first activity is kind of like calisthenics for the intellect. It stirs up the mental air in your head so that words start to float in your mind like leaves falling off trees. Your conscious mind then grabs the words and you write them down.

The activity is called Letter Linkage, and it is similar to word association, but instead of writing down the first word that comes into your mind because of the word you just heard, in Letter Linkage, after you write down an initial word, you examine the letters in that word and then write a second word using some of the letters from the first word. Next, you look at the letters of the second word and use them to come up with a third word. Continuing in this manner, you end up with a column of words where conjoining words share some letters.

The process is described in the following set of instructions, but here I'd like to suggest some of the benefits that seem to accrue from regular practice of this word activity:

1. For one thing, you realize that you know more words than you realize.

2. Second, the more you do this, the more your mind is sensitive to the letter connections between words.

3. Then, when you are writing up a draft (and always draft essays quickly), your mind will alert you to a cogent word that also shares many letters with the word you just wrote down.

4. In this way, you develop consciously a literary dimension to your prose.

5. Another effect of Letter Linkage is that it sensitizes you to the use of words in the texts you read, whether in literature or in science.

6. And because of your heightened sensitivity to the phenomena of words, you might see aspects of the topic that have evaded the author of the text.

7. This activity is one in which the payoff is as much in the practice as it is in the application of the activity in a formal (final draft) setting.

8. In some ways, the activity is like practicing musical scales. Just as a musician won't use scales all the time in performances but the scales might make up certain passages in certain performances, so sometimes when reading you will encounter words with letter linkages and sometimes you will use them in your own writing.

9. At times you may be tempted to construct a sentence with words that share a lot of letters; although it might still express a thought, more often than not such a sentence should not appear in a final draft.

10. Still, it is good to engage with your words in this playful way by constructing sentences that use words from your letter-linkage list.

Instructions for Letter Linkage

- Write a word at the top of a page (any word will do) and then look at the letters of that word and see what new word you can come up that uses several or at least a few letters from that word.

- Write the second word down, just below the first word. (For example, if I wrote *example* at the top of the page, I would look at that word and see the word *ample,* in it, and I would write this below *example.*)

- Then, look at the second word and see if the letters in it can be used to make part of a new word.

- Write the new third word below the second word. (For example, I look at the word *ample,* and I see the word *maple,* so I write that word below *ample.*)

- Try not to spend too much time deciding on a word.

  - The word can be just one letter different—such as going from *like* to *likes.*

  - Use suffixes and prefixes to create new words; that way you won't be stuck in the rut of single-syllable words.

  - Example: The word *cat* could lead to *scat* and then *scattering* and then *tearing* and then *tear* and so on.

- Keep writing down words until you fill in all 20 slots as quickly as possible.

- See how many words you can list in a minute.

- Try to get 20 words in a minute.

- Expect the first few times you do this activity to be rough and clunky. It's a new activity, but with practice it will become easier.

- Vary the kinds of words you start a list with. Begin some lists with one-syllable words, and use more complex words to start other lists.

Here is an example of a Letter Linkage list:

interesting
enter
entertainment
entranced
trance
Transylvania
van
Sylvia
silver
river
rover

over
cove
discover
disco
dissimilar
similar
simian
same
dame

Note: You can also make sentences out of some of the words in the sequence you find them. For example, from this list I came up with this sentence: *We entered an interesting van near the river called Sylvia, and discovered disco was quite dissimilar from anything the silver simians were concocting!*

The Word–Image Dynamic

The Presence of Images in the Phenomena of Words

Here is something I want you to dwell on now and later and often: Ordinarily, adults (i.e., people) think with words, but what they don't realize is that often these **words trigger images in their minds** and often their thinking through of a problem or a challenge to their convictions is just a reaction to images triggered by the words used in the thinking experience. They don't realize that their fear of change is prompted by a fear that the image will be changed. Often, too, the images are from childhood and so have two weaknesses: (1) they are simplistic and (2) they carry emotional baggage.

This claim is not something I've come up with on my own. Back in 1957, Northrop Frye, in his landmark study called *The Anatomy of Criticism*, noted, "It is impossible to read the word 'cat' in a context without some representational flash of the animal so named" (74).

On the inside front cover of this textbook there is a diagram of this verbal phenomena. Notice that whether the word is spoken or read, it triggers images in the adult mind, and those images come from either an overt metaphor or a non-metaphor word. Later in the chapter, you will do some activities related to the two origins of images.

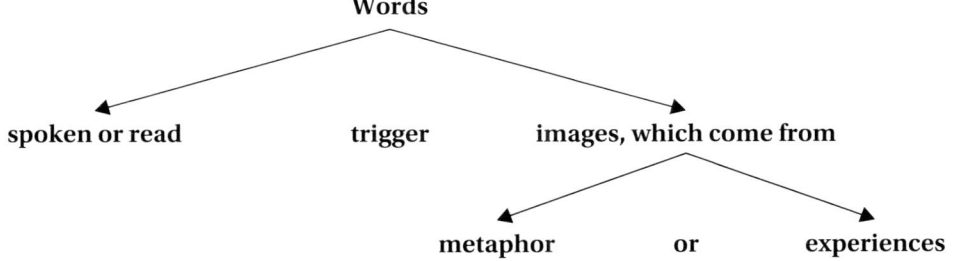

Distinguishing Metaphors from Similes

First, let me clarify what we are not looking for: we are not looking for similes, which are comparisons between different things in which the word *as* or *like* is used in the comparison. Often we get ideas for metaphors from similes, but the simile isn't the big game that we are after.

For example, here is a simile:

He ate like a pig.

Note: The word *pig* triggered an image in your head, but the word *pig* is not being used as a metaphor because *like* is in front of it. The comparison implies that the two things are separate: He *ate like* a pig, but he is not actually a pig.

Here is a metaphor from this simile:

He pigs out.

Note: Involved in this example is what we call the "identification" or "equivalency" of the metaphor; the sentence implies that the human is an actual pig—at least in character if not physical form, psychically or emotionally (and so intellectually), but not concretely.

In both cases, the sentences create strong images of pigs in the reader's mind, and the nature and extent of those images are dependent on each individual's personal experiences. The words "pig" and "pigs" both generate concrete images, although those images may—and likely do—differ among individuals.

Think of it this way: to describe psychological events, things that are intangible but have a reality that is genuine, we use metaphors; we draw upon physical things to make such realities concrete, give them substance, and give them some kind of tangibility. The following diagram further clarifies the point:

Metaphors
Physical events phrased as metaphors help us describe:

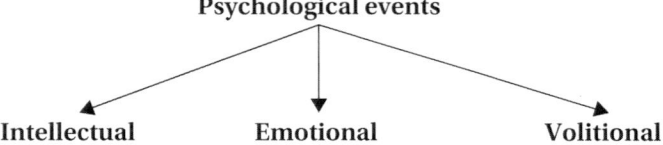

Here is a very important insight to take from this chapter: the human mind uses metaphors automatically to explain facts and truths and to describe things. Once you understand the adult mind's automatic use of metaphors, you will begin to use metaphors deliberately in your prose, and you will be more sensitive to the presence of metaphors in the things that you read and hear. You will also take time to explore how metaphors could be used to help you write explanations that are more accurate and precise than those you have written in the past when you were not so conscious of metaphors.

Using Metaphors as Critical Thinking Tools

Consider the following sentences:

1. Science is a spotlight on reality.

2. Science spotlights a part of reality.

In the first sentence, the logic of the wording implies that science is an actual physical spotlight, illuminating reality. I would encourage you to at first take this imagery very literally (what I now call *physically literally*, for reasons you will soon see). You can use this feature when wondering if a word is being used metaphorically or not by asking yourself, *Am I supposed to imagine that this thing is physically what is being said here?* In the case of the example sentence, then, you would ask, *Am I supposed to believe that I can find an actual spotlight that says "science" on it and **is** "science"?* For now, take the sentence at "face" value, and read on.

Here is another feature of the metaphor–image dynamic to consider regarding the example sentence: What kind of spotlight do you see? It's been my experience that most students see a single spotlight from the rafters of a theater stage, although often enough students see a spotlight like those used by police officers (I wonder why!), or a light tower. But in all cases, I think the following dynamic, discussed more fully in the rest of the chapter, occurs: Whatever the specific image, the image of the spotlight can be very valuable in suggesting something about the phenomena of science that "plain" (non-metaphorical) wording would not be able to do.

To further illustrate this point, the following drawing is an image that most students would say is a faithful rendering of the imagery provoked by the second sentence "Science spotlights a part of reality." (In some ways, "a part of" is redundant in the sentence, as spotlights by definition cover only a small area, but I just want to get a specific image into the reader's mind.) Here is the image I created:

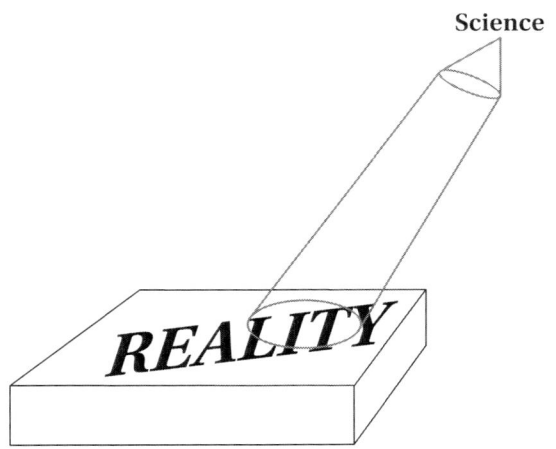

Here, the word *reality* is spelled across the stage (or is the stage) and part of that word is being illuminated by the spotlight named "science." The word *science* likely triggered in your mind images of specific scientists, or images of your own experiences with science. Perhaps you saw images from movies about science. But because the sentence uses "science spotlights," the metaphor is directing you to see a spotlight, and to see the practice of science as that spotlight. The sense of the sentence is that only a part of reality is illuminated by science. (The statement could be rephrased or clarified as "Science spotlights just a part of reality.")

In either case, here is the important point: This image (science as spotlight) can prompt a series of questions, and **these questions constitute critical thinking.** Here are a few questions that might arise as you study the drawing:

1. If science illuminates just a part of reality, can the spotlight be widened to illuminate a larger part? If so, what does that mean in the actual practice or experience of science? These questions might then prompt the following thoughts:

    a. Are more experiments needed?

    b. What are current scientists working on? Are some areas currently being ignored or are underrepresented in the field of science?

    c. Are there other parts of reality, beyond the part illuminated by science, in which someone could become expert or that could be better understood through study?

2. It seems natural to then ask the question: Can other spotlights be turned on? Which in turn prompts the following thoughts:

    a. Another spotlight would have to be something totally different from science. Is there anything that is contrasted with science in the popular mind?

    b. Art is often considered to be the contrast or opposite of science.

3. Considering art as this other spotlight, how can it be represented on the diagram?

    a. Because art is often considered to be very different from science, a very different way of understanding reality, the spotlight called art could be placed on the other side of the stage, opposite science.

    b. Because college has traditionally divided its disciplines into the arts and the sciences, the art spotlight could be placed at the same height as the science spotlight to suggest that they have equal value.

4. Now, here's a question that leads to reflection and discussion: Would the art spotlight illuminate the same section of reality that science spotlights?

    a. Some might say that art will illuminate a different section of reality, as represented in the following illustration:

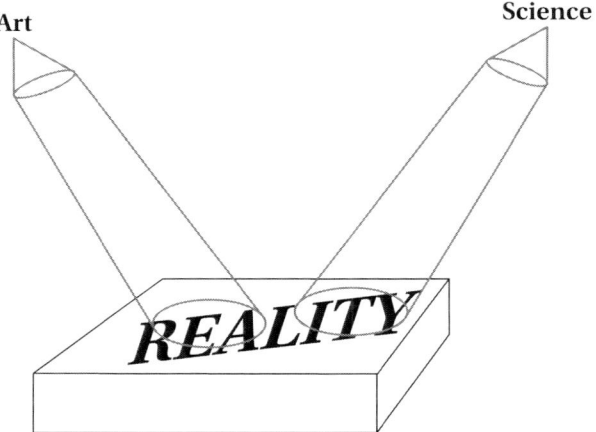

b. This illustration suggests that art and science illuminate different aspects of reality, and they can't find ways to interact fruitfully with each other.

5. What if, instead, the art spotlight is placed in the illustration so that it is shining from the other side onto the same area illuminated by science? The revised illustration is as follows:

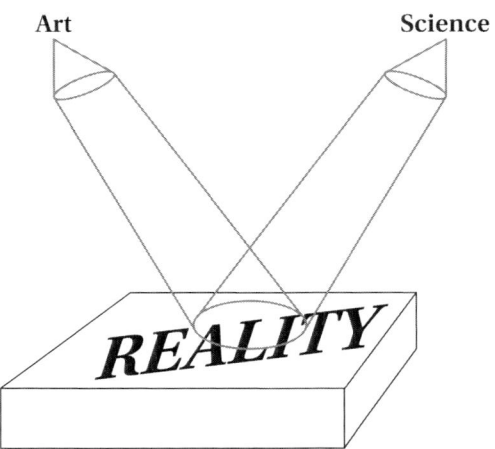

a. This suggests that art and science can illuminate the same section of reality.

6. Which illustration is more valid?

a. What tests could validate each claim or suggest that it is mistaken?

This is an example **examining the implications and entailments** caused by the image triggered in your mind by the words in the sentence. Word–image analysis is a valuable part of critical thinking skills. When you examine the mental activity triggered by the sentence, you are able to see more aspects of the actuality and reality represented by its words and images. In this way, you are engaged more deeply with your use of words and images, and with practice, your mind becomes more sensitive to the use of metaphors in the texts you read. In addition, you will see that imagination influences the quality of your critical thinking.

Images Triggered by Non-Metaphor Words

The spotlight example shows the work of an *overt* or *living metaphor*. Images can also be triggered by words that are not overt images, but are key words in our lives. For example, the word *God* triggers images in people's minds, and is a significant, or key, word in many people's lives. When I see that word, the images in my mind are of Michelangelo's painting of God on the ceiling of the Sistine Chapel. Most Westerners have seen this painting, so the word *God* may trigger that same image for many U.S. adults. For others, different images might accompany the word *God*, but all images—regardless of their differing content—come from childhood, from religious upbringing and from the general culture, especially its media outlets.

Critical thinkers must then ask, *Is that image really a good representation of what God is actually like?* In most cases, the image—from childhood—is not likely to reflect a realistic portrayal or understanding of God (if there is a God, the cautious might assert).

Imaginary Realism or Imaginative Realism?

When adults (and, yes, college students, young adults in their late teens and early 20s) do not examine this word–image dynamic, they have a sense of realism that could be called "imaginary realism." (Northrop Frye uses a term that is a bit more abrasive—"stupid realism"—but I won't go that far!) As a result, their solutions for society's grave problems are unrealistic, sterile, and imaginary—not imaginative but imaginary. In contrast, becoming aware of this word–image dynamic and engaging more deeply with words and their images results in the ability to distinguish the imaginary idea from the imaginative idea. This causes a shift from inadequate adult engagement with words to a more-than-adequate adult engagement with words.

Along with this shift comes the realization that some images need to be scrubbed from the constellation of images triggered by key words, as they are inadequate vestiges from childhood. Adult emotions will continue to be affected by images from childhood if these images are not recognized as inadequate—possessed by a realism that is imaginary and not imaginative. And I hasten to add that even when thinking is at the level of imaginative realism, certain aspects of the external world still will cause anxiety. However, those anxieties are not the result of inadequate adult engagement with words and the images triggered by those words that really have no basis in the objective, external world. It is true that real-enough anxieties are triggered by imaginary realism, but the result is that the imaginary prompts such thinkers to act in ways that they (and others) later regret.

Concluding Remarks

1. When you examine the images triggered in your mind by the words you and others use, your thinking becomes visceral as well as cerebral.

2. This examination of the images conjured up in your mind by the words you see and use allows you to express yourself in wording that is more accurate and precise.

3. If you can achieve an adult-level engagement with metaphors, you have taken the first steps toward achieving an adult-level engagement with words and the understanding of words, other aspects of college-level thinking that will be explored in due season.

4. College-level thinking isn't necessarily academic thinking, but it is adult-level thinking. It is important to make that distinction. Both Joe Civilian and Jane Academic should have a college-level engagement with words (CLEW).

5. You will see that because you have been using metaphors automatically (without much consideration or examination) in your prose, there is a literary dimension already present in your regular writing.

6. When you begin to examine the metaphors you use and then use them deliberately, you will likely realize distinctions and clarifications that you have not seen before, thus deepening your understanding.

Letter Linkage Sessions

NAME: ....

DATE: ....

CLASS HOUR: ....

Session 1 Starting Word:	Session 2 Starting Word:
1.	
2.	
3.	
4.	
5.	
6.	
7.	
8.	
9.	
10.	
11.	
12.	
13.	
14.	
15.	
16.	
17.	
18.	
19.	
20.	

Session 1 Time Elapsed:_____   Session 2 Time Elapsed:_____

Thoughts:

....

....

....

....

....

Use as many words in your lists as you can to write some sentences. The sentences should be grammatically correct, but they don't need to make sense. Just play with the language.

Write two sentences using the words from Session 1:

1.

2.

Write two sentences using the words from Session 2:

1.

2.

Exploring the Images of a Metaphor: Sword

NAME: ....   CLASS HOUR: ....   DATE: ....

Consider this sentence as you answer the following questions:

Because it is claimed that the pen is mightier than the sword, perhaps, then, the word is the mightiest sword.

First-Tier Questions

1. What words in the sentence are to be taken physically literally?

2. What words in the sentence are not to be taken physically literally?

3. Describe the images in your mind caused by the metaphorical words.

4. What entailments can be deduced from the sword metaphor? For instance, how would you sharpen this sword? Would different swords be used for different academic disciplines?

5. What time period is your imagery in? Could you come up with imagery for a different time period? How would that affect the ideas about writing that you got from your original imagery?

Exploring the Images of a Metaphor: Womb

NAME: .... CLASS HOUR: .... DATE: ....

Consider this sentence as you answer the following questions:

At birth we are physically born into a verbal environment, and our culture is so verbal that it is like we are in a verbal womb when we enter college.

First-Tier Questions

1. What words in the sentence are to be taken physically literally?

2. What words in the sentence are not to be taken physically literally?

3. Describe the images in your mind caused by the metaphorical words.

4. What entailments can be deduced from the womb and birthing metaphor? For instance, what would the doctor be in the college environment? The nurse?

5. What time period is your imagery in? Could you come up with imagery for a different time period? How would that affect the ideas about writing that you got from your original imagery?

Exploring the Images of a Metaphor: Birth

Consider this sentence as you answer the following questions:

He birthed the idea, but I provided the warm waters of revision.

(Note the incongruence of the physical imagery but the rightness of the intellectual imagery—either gender pop those babies out quickly.)

First-Tier Questions

1. What words in the sentence are to be taken physically literally?

2. What terms in the sentence are not to be taken physically literally?

3. Describe the images in your mind caused by the metaphorical words.

4. What entailments can be deduced from the birthing metaphor? For instance, could there be cold waters that resulted in something other than revision?

5. What time period is your imagery in? Could you come up with imagery for a different time period? How would that affect the ideas about writing that you got from your original imagery?

Exploring the Images of a Metaphor: Singing

NAME: .... CLASS HOUR: .... DATE: ....

Consider this sentence as you answer the following questions:

My pen sang as I wrote down words that shared the same vowels.

First-Tier Questions

1. What words in the sentence are to be taken physically literally?

2. What words in the sentence are not to be taken physically literally?

3. Describe the images in your mind caused by the words.

4. Examine the images you described and come up with other imagery dealing with the content. For example:

   a. If you saw the ballpoint as being the mouth out of which comes song, could that mouth be elsewhere on the pen?

   b. What kind of pen did you see? Could you see a different pen?

5. What time period is your imagery in? Could you come up with imagery for a different time period? How would that affect the ideas about writing that you got from your original imagery?

6. Could the mouth be talking to you? The pen talks to you? What would it say or could say want to say about you and your engagement with words?

Exploring the Images of a Metaphor: Tugboat

NAME: .... CLASS HOUR: .... DATE: ....

Consider this sentence as you answer the following questions:

The tugboat of proofreading steered the ship of my essay into the dock of final form.

First-Tier Questions

1. What words in the sentence are to be taken physically literally?

2. What terms in the sentence are not to be taken physically literally?

3. Describe the images in your mind caused by the metaphorical words.

4. What entailments can be deduced from the boat and harbor metaphor? For instance, what would the dock workers be in the writing environment? The cranes on the dock?

5. What time period is your imagery in? Could you come up with imagery for a different time period? How would that affect the ideas about writing that you got from your original imagery?

Non-Metaphor Words That Trigger Images: Part 1

NAME: .... CLASS HOUR: .... DATE: ....

BACKGROUND—It is essential to slow down the thinking process that occurs with words or that words facilitate, and to recognize that words trigger images and that these images come from metaphors and/or experiences. In this activity, you will describe images that non-metaphorical words trigger in your mind.

ACTIVITY—After you read each of the following words, close your eyes and notice what image is triggered by the word. The image might have some activity, motion, or fluidity to it. It is just as likely that the image will be static, an image frozen like a painting. Whatever is, is, so there is no right or wrong here. Write down a description of that image. CAUTION: Be careful that you aren't writing what the words mean. Expect these words to trigger images in your mind based on your experience, and describe those images.

God:

Criticism:

Devil:

Jesus:

Buddha:

Social Media:

Education:

Non-Metaphor Words That Trigger Images: Part 2

NAME: .... CLASS HOUR: .... DATE: ....

ACTIVITY—Using the principle of contrast, decide what would be the opposite image of the one that was triggered in your mind in Part 1 by each word in the following list. Take care that you make exact correspondences. For example, to say that the opposite of God is the devil is not correct. Examine the image you wrote in Part 1 and consider the contrast to each element in your description. So, for example, if part of your description of God was that he is strong, you would now consider the contrasting image—he is weak.

The exploration of images triggered by words shouldn't cause anxiety just because you are examining words that you were told during your childhood were important. Part of getting to an adult understanding involves detaching the images from words we learned in childhood, and seeing both the limits and genius of those images.

God:

Criticism:

Devil:

Jesus:

Buddha:

Social Media:

Education:

CHAPTER 3

The Writing Process

The domination of print in Western society...has created all the conditions of freedom within that society: democracy and [literacy] are interdependent. *(Northrop Frye, The Critical Path 151)*

Goals:

- See the writing process as perfect because it allows messiness at first and forgives early errors.
- Clarify the attitudes and assumptions proper to the stages of the writing process.

Outcomes:

- Change assumptions and attitudes about writing process.
- Prize the revision of a first draft more than the writing of a first draft.
- Develop a deeper engagement with the writing process so the entire process is play.

Terms to Know:

- Durable and situational expectations
- Play and work attitudes
- Fracturing a paragraph
- Flush-left diagramming

Rationale

It's been my experience that when students get a writing assignment, they are less than happy to engage in this process. This suggests to me a need to examine the attitudes that students bring to the writing process, along with an examination of their understanding of the phenomena of words and the level of their engagement with words. This chapter begins with an examination of the assumptions that I've often seen in first-year college students. It then moves to an examination of the proper attitudes and assumptions that belong with each stage of the writing process. I have placed this chapter early in the book because (1) this is a book on college-level writing and (2) I hope students use this chapter for their writing assignments in other courses that they are taking right now. The following are assumptions and attitudes that inexperienced students use but that they need to drop:

Assumptions Inexperienced Writers Must Drop

1. They have to have thoughts before they start writing.

2. They have to understand their topic before writing about it.

3. They think problems indicate a lack of ability.

4. They think they have to spend a lot of time on the first draft.

5. They often invest too much value in first draft.

6. They think after the first draft their next concern is spelling/grammar.

7. They can't bring a sense of play or experimentation to the writing task—it must be serious.

Instead, the following assumptions and attitudes must be embraced by student writers:

Assumptions and Attitudes That Inexperienced Writers Must Embrace

1. Although it would be nice to have thoughts before beginning to write, because thinking is largely done with words, if they write words down, this will get the gears of thinking moving.

2. Although it is good to understand a topic before beginning to write, this isn't entirely necessary, and experienced writers know that they will develop their understanding of the topic during revision.

3. Problems are inevitable and force the writer to become a problem solver and a detective, uncovering the best solutions to problems of organization and word choice.

4. Because the first draft is expected to be rough, it is also expected that not much of the first draft will get into the final draft—so, the first draft should be written quickly. That way, students won't feel so invested in the wording that any revisions are resisted, as they didn't labor over it to "birth" it.

5. It is best not to invest much of the self in the first draft, and to prevent this from happening, it helps to write drafts quickly, and do revision activities more slowly.

6. Because sentences might be removed from a draft for a variety of reasons, don't bother with spelling and grammar during early revisions. Instead, first look at the larger picture of organization and content.

7. Because students have a living relationship with their language— something that I hope college shows students how to get (and which this book seeks to develop in students)—they write to see what happens, expecting their words to lead them to new insights about the things they are most familiar with.

Never More These Two Things

It is my hope that two things will **no longer happen** as a result of students examining and taking ownership of these attitudes and assumptions:

1. No longer will you stare at the screen or paper for more than 30 seconds—wondering what you will write—before you start writing.

2. You will never, ever again be negative about the roughness of your first attempts (which means your internal critic is not only on vacation, but—as negativity—it is permanently disabled, perhaps even annihilated).

I'm not trying to replace your writing method but to complement it, add onto it, and improve it. If you have a process that lessens anxiety from the get-go, keep using it. If you find that depression or anxiety is your first reaction to a writing assignment, or that you spend a long time just staring at a computer screen wondering what to write, then I'd encourage you to test this method that likely will increase your chances of producing a stellar final written document.

Overview of the Stages of the Writing Process

Following is an outline of the stages of the writing process. After you read through it, you will find my further glosses on each step. In the outline, the size of the word suggests how important the stage is.

The Stages of Writing
1. Invention
2. First draft
3. Revision
   A. Global revision
   B. Sentence revision
4. Editing
5. Proofreading

Two General Attitudes Used in the Writing Process
Play and Work

Attitude of Play Dominant in These Stages
Invention and First Draft

Attitude of Work Dominant in These Stages
Revision, Editing, and Proofreading

Traits of the Play Attitude

1. You do not judge the quality of any of your thoughts when you are first generating ideas for your assignment.
2. You expect your first jottings to be weak or confused or clunky.
3. You write from the heart.
4. You write for yourself.
5. You want to generate a lot of writing: Quantity is more important at this time than quality of ideas or of the writing.
6. You expect your writing to help you discover what you think about a topic.
7. You believe that writing causes thinking.
8. You lower your expectations about producing good stuff at the first try.
9. You abandon the idea that you have to understand the topic before you write about it.

10. You stop assuming that your best ideas have to occur to you before you start writing, and assume that the writing will lead you to your best ideas.

Activities of Invention Using the Play Attitude

1. There are specific methods of invention that you can find in any online writing site.

2. Or, "just write"; you may find that a stream of ideas occurs to you.

3. Even when you have no thoughts in your head, just write. I use the following process:

    a. First, I will just write this: "I have no thoughts about this topic."

    b. Usually a thought will emerge while I am writing that sentence.

    c. If not, then I often write a description of my goals or assignment: "I'm supposed to write about my assumptions about education. I've never thought about it. The teacher feels . . . "

    d. Then I find that I begin to write a lot. It might not all be good, but at the invention level, I'm just getting words out, and not being critical of the writing.

    e. I just "pop those babies out" quickly so I'm not too attached to them.

4. Write in sentence form as much as possible, but phrases and single words are fine as well.

5. Write quickly so that you can get past the cliché stuff and get to your own personal take on things.

6. Expect the subconscious to be organizing your data as you write it down.

7. If you find yourself not writing, and instead wondering if you should write this or that, tell yourself that you have a good question, and then write it all down—write about your writing and thinking—and see what happens.

8. At some point, do some Letter Linkage activities (see Chapter 2) on key words.

9. At some point, identify key words and the images they trigger in your mind. Write down a description of the images and reflect on what other images could the words trigger in the minds of readers.

FIRST DRAFT

1. If you write a lot at the invention stage, your mind will begin to subconsciously organize your thoughts.

2. First, make a brief outline, OR just write, and continue to use the assumptions and attitudes of invention.

3. Write quickly, so you don't get too attached to the writing: pop those babies out quickly.

4. Writers tend to not want to give up what they labor over, and so they are less willing to "abort" their "babies" during revision.

5. If you write fast, you will find it easier to delete parts of what you have written.

   The more your write, the more you realize that you have other ideas to replace the "darlings" that you deleted.

6. You still write mostly for quantity, not for quality. It will be easier to delete sentences in revision than to create them.

7. Continue to consider drafting to be a process of discovering new thoughts.

8. If new thoughts occur to you, write them down in this draft, or start a different page titled "Thoughts while drafting," and then get back to your original design (rough though it may be).

9. Remember, we call a first draft "rough" for a reason. So don't expect a "rough" draft to be polished!

10. If your first draft is rough, then that is perfect!

REVISION

Traits of the Work Attitude

1. You start to judge the quality of your writing style (and later, the quality of your thoughts).

2. You start using the Principles of Reader Expectations (PRE—described in Chapter 5) to identify the relative condition of sentences and paragraphs.

3. You revise with the head now, not with the heart.

4. You write for the reader now, more than yourself.

5. You are concerned about the quality and clarity of writing (and later, the quality of the ideas).

6. Still, you expect revision to help you discover what you think about a topic.

7. You still believe that writing causes thinking.

8. You raise your expectations, believing that you will shape the draft into good material.

9. You know that your writing (especially revision) will develop your understanding of the topic. Maybe some research is necessary, but your mind can educate you sometimes, and in very good ways, when you just write.

Activities of Revision Using the Work Attitude

Durable and Situational Expectations: The revision stage is the **most important part of the Perfect Writing Process,** but inexperienced writers don't know this. Or they do the **wrong** stuff in revision.

The Perfect Writing Process wants you to revise your draft through your reader's eyes. The phrase "revising through your readers' eyes" has perplexed students in the past—they wonder how they could see through another person's eyes—but you will be able to revise through the reader's eyes when you understand the concepts about the phenomena of words (see Chapter 2) and PRE.

So as you begin the revision process, remember that

1. Words automatically trigger images in the readers' mind; and

2. Readers have expectations about sentences that do not pertain to grammar, but are prompted by grammatically correct sentences.

You can think of "reader expectations" as occurring on two levels, durable expectations and situational, as follows:

- **Durable level:** These are reader expectations dealing with the structures of sentences and paragraphs. To address them, you identify the location of subjects and verbs (which both civilian and academic readerships agree on) and you describe the identities of subjects and verbs (where the two readerships can diverge).

- **Situational level:** These are expectations generated by the specific words you use. To address them, you have to study what images will be triggered by your key words, which first appear in the title. You also anticipate if the reader will appreciate each word (for its imagery or meaning) or not, and then decide if the word will remain (and thus risk rejection by the reader) or not.

Global Revision

In the global revision stage, you look at the organization of the ideas; you want to get a sense of the essay's whole structure.

I. First, read to get a feel for the **general trajectory** of the text—a sense of its parts, and the length of each section.

    a. Determine the major sections of the body of the essay.

        i. Determine when the opening ends.

            1. Do you have an effective opening hook?

        ii. Determine when the closing starts.

            1. Realize that often the closing echoes the opening.

        iii. Note whether the title gives a focus to the text. (See the following section on titles., under "Audience Appeal").

    b. ON A SEPARATE SHEET OF PAPER, list your "contracts" (formerly called *topic sentences*) and ask:

        i. Would the reader know why you present stuff in the order it's in?

        ii. Do the contracts contain key words from the thesis or words that allude to the thesis (if you have one)?

        iii. Do you have an effective order of key points?

            1. Going from most familiar to least familiar (or vice versa)

            2. Going from most important to least important (or vice versa)

            3. Going from least complex to most complex (or vice versa)

    c. Do you use **transitional words that mark the start of a new section?**

        i. Would the reader be able to identify key words repeated as part of a transition to a new section?

        ii. Can you use words like *next*, or *second* to make any transitions clearer?

II. Focus on content development: Are the ideas all fully explained? Is there extra stuff you can drop?

    a. Does each paragraph have a contract, and do sentences following it link to the contract?

    b. Do the sentences in the paragraph following the contract use *old-to-new* information flow, which results in coherence and cohesion?

    c. A key concern is a sense of proportion:

      i.   Do you spend the right amount of "time" on the various aspects of your topic?

      ii.   Determine how many paragraphs are devoted to each point.

  d. What kinds of evidence/details are given?

      i.   Do you rely on personal observation?

      ii.   Do you use expert opinion?

      iii.   Do you use empirical studies or humanities scholarship?

      iv.   Do you use evidence from popular culture?

      v.   Do you use any other kinds of evidence?

      vi.   Does rhetorical wordplay help drive a point home?

  e. A key analytical concept is to look for **contrasts,** for opposites being explored:

      i.   Can you explain your idea using contrasting metaphors or images?

      ii.   Can you accurately describe views you will oppose or refute?

      iii.   Can you show contrasts using words that share many of the same letters?

      iv.   Sometimes the contrasts aren't opposites but distinctions that clarify our understanding of the issue—can you convey this in your draft?

SENTENCE REVISION

1. You look at the **efficiency** of each sentence using PRE, and you are looking at the **effectiveness** of word choices and sentence structures.

2. IN OTHER WORDS: You are NOT looking at the correctness of grammar.

3. You examine the sentence structures to be sure that they meet reader expectations:

  a. Determine if your readership is civilian or academic, which will influence the kinds of verbs you will employ. (Remember, though, that both and all readerships have the same preferences for locations of subjects and verbs.)

  b. Identify if the verb voice is active or passive. (Vague writing often uses the passive voice **too often** and unnecessarily.)

c. Identify whether the subjects of verbs are persons or nominalizations. (Nominalizations used too often in the subject position can result in writing that doesn't get traction in the reader's mind.)

d. Identify the contract of each paragraph and determine if the sentences following it observe the contract.

e. Identify whether familiar information begins sentences.

f. If you identify places where you are violating reader expectations (PRE), you can justify the violations in terms of rhetorical needs or to observe old-to-new information flow, or for other good reason.

g. Identify those sentence structures that can *never* be considered strong, regardless of rhetorical needs, and revise it before the reader can notice your lack of awareness of what you have produced on the page.

4. You examine your word choices to see if they make the reader think of stuff you had not intended.

a. This can happen when you try to be vivid.

b. Metaphors can conjure up images in the reader's mind that you did not anticipate.

c. At the sentence-revision stage, make sure to consider all the possible images that the key metaphors can produce.

5. Many of the issues at the sentence-revision level might be addressed when you are examining a paragraph for contract observances.

6. NOTE AGAIN: Sentence mechanics dealing with grammar and punctuation are NOT a concern of the revision stage of the Perfect Writing Process.

Audience Appeal

1. Will your **title** bring a smile or a look of interest to the reader's face?

a. Can you put a Letter Linkage pun in the title?

b. Can you use a two-part title?

c. Do you want key words from the assignment put into the title?

d. Do any words in the title trigger images in your mind?

   i. Do you want words in the title to trigger images in the reader's mind?

   ii. Do you want those images triggered in the reader's mind?

   iii. Those images set up expectations in the reader's mind about what he or she will read in the introduction—does your introduction meet those expectations or leave the reader wondering what you are doing?

2. In the **introduction,** what rhetorical device do you use to grab the reader's attention?

   a. Do you ask a question, tell a story, make an observation, or use wordplay?

   b. What expectations does the intro create in your reader?

   c. Does the next paragraph meet the reader's expectations?

   d. What expectations does the wording in the opening paragraph create in the reader's mind that the reader expects will be met in the next paragraph(s)?

   e. Does the opening paragraph meet the expectations of the assignment?

   f. Do you want to put key words from the assignment into the opening paragraph?

3. What metaphors are you using automatically?

   a. Do you want to explore using one or two of these deliberately?

   b. Can you find a metaphor that would be greeted with relish by the audience?

Rewriting in Response to Revision Analysis

Attitudes:

1. You return to your play and discovery attitudes.

2. You are not worried about getting the wording or structure right the first time you redraft a passage.

3. You just write possible solutions to the problems that you have identified.

4. Indeed, with practice, you understand how the entire writing process is really one of play and discovery, testing and exploration.

Assumptions:

1. You understand that your revision activities are helping you re-see your experience in new ways, helpful ways.

2. Also, readers don't know that some of the best insights they read in your final draft occurred to you during revision, unless you tell them that in your final draft!

3. You expect that your understanding of your topic will deepen as you revise for PRE at the sentence and paragraph levels.

4. You also assume that more external research will improve your understanding.

5. You understand that you don't need a big vocabulary to write at the adult level (i.e., college level), but you can see possibilities in the words already on the page.

6. The text you present will have the reader not just read a page of words but a page of objects, or images popping up from key words, whether they are metaphors or not.

Activities

Note: For specific ways to revise sentences or paragraphs in need of rehabilitation, see the chapters on sentences and on paragraphs. Some activities this textbook encourages students to consider are the following:

1. Flush-left diagramming (FLD) of sentences for observance of subject–verb expectations

2. Concerns about subjects and verbs:
   a. Determine if the verb is as vivid as it needs to be.
   b. See if converting infinitives into verbs makes the content stronger.
   c. See if you are overusing "be" verbs as main verbs or other verbs that don't convey much action (e.g., *had, seems, does, says*).
      i. See if you can eliminate 50 percent of the "be" verbs you use.
      ii. That is, rewrite those sentences so they don't have "be" verbs in them and see if those sentences sound better and convey the information more effectively.
   d. Make sure you haven't overused nominalizations in the subject position.
   e. Make sure you haven't overused the passive voice unnecessarily.
   f. Perhaps convert active voice verbs (AVV) to passive voice verbs (PVV) and vice versa.

3. Fracturing of paragraphs for observance of contract and old-to-new concepts
   a. Pay attention to short paragraphs, those with three or fewer sentences.
   b. Combining fracturing (also called "fragging") with FLD increases the likelihood that you will be able to explain why your paragraph was "lame-o" and why it is now "dressed to the nines."

4. This attention to PRE could also become a new global focus, because it doesn't concern itself with grammar and syntax, issues that editing would focus on at the sentence level. PRE deals with expectations readers have about the functions of words within sentences.

5. Comb through all the grammatical subjects and their verbs early on, because they act as the two claws that can grab the reader's attention and don't let go.

6. In addition, when you give this attention just to subjects and verbs, often you might then see aspects of the topic that had been hidden, and these aspects might constitute new content, which is a concern of traditional global revision.

Final Reflection on the Revision Stage

1. The revision stage is the transformation stage.

2. It is the clarification stage and the differentiation stage.

3. It is the fulcrum stage where you pivot from wording that isn't very accurate and precise to wording that is precise and accurate, from wording that is rough and organization that is messy into wording that is polished and organization that is imaginatively structured.

4. You should expect some of the best ideas in your final draft to have occurred to you during revision.

5. When you experiment with metaphors during the invention and revision stages of the writing/thinking process, you are really developing a sense of a living language, and you will become more intellectually awake to words that you hear, speak, read, and write.

Editing

1. Here is where you work on grammar.

2. It's been my experience that grammar is what students erroneously focus on in revision.

3. They sense that their ideas are incomplete, and they think that grammar will help them complete ideas.

   a. When a passage is correct in grammar, but incomplete in thought, and students don't see that (only sense it), they think they can't write.

   b. A sentence can be grammatically correct but still not efficient or effective.

4. So don't obsess over grammar until this stage.

5. It's also been my experience that many grammatical glitches are fixed when examining subject–verb combinations in the light of reader expectations.

6. Then, if the revision process has worked, your writing will disclose not just rehashed ideas, but new ideas generated by the process.

   a. The essay might have a dynamic within the writing that causes the reader to come up with new thoughts.

   b. These thoughts complete or complement what you wrote, which is stimulating to the reader.

   c. That kind of experience would leave the reader very unconcerned about grammar glitches.

7. But try not to have any grammar glitches!

Proofreading

1. You are not looking to develop ideas or organize them.

2. You are not looking at grammar and mechanics.

3. You are looking for surface typos and punctuation errors.

4. And a good way to find these is to read your writing backwards.

Just Remember:

- William Stafford says that for the person who trusts and forgives him- or herself, the process of writing becomes a liberating experience.

- Do not be overly judgmental in the first stages of writing.

- Just relax, write, explore, and play, and expect new ideas to emerge from your own mind.

- It might take time to trust the process, but it's like weight lifting—you don't see results for months.

- Hopefully you see results immediately. If you just write, test out options, and realize that questions are as important to the advancement of self-understanding and knowledge as answers, you could find this writing thing to be very interesting.

CONCLUDING THOUGHTS

In the textbook I used to use in class, the first statement—printed in boldface text—read, "Writing is hard work." It has been my experience that if you follow the attitudes and assumptions outlined in this chapter, the entire process eventually becomes easy and stimulating from the get-go. What becomes difficult is managing your time in order for you to do justice to the rich inner life that is growing inside of you and is aching to get "heard" through your writing.

One thing that I've found is that if I begin a sentence and feel that it isn't going anywhere, sometimes I'll just keep writing through the chunkiness, and within a sentence or two I feel like I'm on more solid ground. Often I will realize–or my brain will tell me—that I've not written down a main verb even though I've written seven or eight words. That means I will need to revise that sentence. I will then stop, make a mark to signal I'm starting over (I write: . . . ???. . .), then begin a revision of that sentence, but now with a verb stated early in the sentence. And sometimes I'm deleting a thought I find clever, but I have to be severely critical of my writing, which means I have to understand that what I find clever is likely to fall flat in the reader's "ear."

Eventually, you realize that because thinking is largely done with words, and you are engaged with words at the invention and revision level, the final draft has content that occurred to you in the invention and revision stage. Therefore, the entire process is one of play.

CHAPTER 4

College-Level Reading in the Light of Imaginative Literacy and the Two Readerships

The arts of the trivium have been rechristened as reading, writing and thinking. [Although these] new terms leave an impression more literary than intellectual, [they are meant to prepare one] to read a text of objects no less than a page of letters. (Mark Van Doren, *Liberal Education* 82)

Goals:

- Understand unique aspects of academic writing.
- Understand the reading methods for essays and for books.

Outcomes:

- Explain why a text doesn't get traction in the student mind.
- Demonstrate the use of a reading process to unpack difficult academic writing.

Terms to Know:

- Nominalizations
- Passive-voice verbs
- Quantification of text

Introduction

The quotation from Mark Van Doren that opens this paragraph underscores a key goal of this text, which is to get students to not just read words on the page but to perceive objects popping out of the words on the page. His statements also underscore the importance of reading for the person who wants an adult understanding of things.

It is presumed that his comments make sense only after the student has engaged with words at the enlightened adult level. The student reaches this level of engagement with words by being aware of the word–image dynamic and by using metaphors intentionally. With this understanding, students are now sensitive to the images triggered in their minds by words; because they now have consciously-triggered images accompanying metaphors, they will now expect to read a page of images and objects while they read a page of words.

One thing I want to stress in this chapter is that reading at the college level isn't necessarily the same as reading (and writing) at the academic level. College-level reading is adult, permanent, and imaginative. College-level reading is linked to the needs of an educated electorate in a democracy. It is paramount that all college students achieve this permanent level of reading (which will never become an obsolete method of reading), a level that is adult, enlightened, and imaginative. This level of reading applies to both civilian and academic readers.

Of course, there is overlap between the readerships of the civilian and the academic. The academic is a civilian outside the college campus, but as an academic, the scholar has preferences about word choice relative to subject and verb identities in texts that are written for academic audiences. These differences have been addressed in chapters 5 and 6, and the reader should consult those chapters as needed.

In addition, the academic is often analyzing the institutions that the civilian resides in, but with one crucial difference: after college, the student will now have a job for 40+ years in commercial civilization's economic institutions. And most students assume that college is important for improving their chances of getting a "good" job. (Of course, the academic is in this economic structure too, and the institution of liberal education is affected by the economic cycles as well.)

Now, the academic is critically examining these institutions of commercial civilization with critical thinking methods that the civilian should be using, but when the academic presents the fruits of his or her intellectual labors, in written or verbal form, he or she will be addressing an academic audience, an audience that has specific preferences with regard to subject and verb identities (apart from issues of vocabulary and jargon). For instance, consider this sentence from John Henry Newman:

> It is obvious that the first step which faculty have to effect in the conversion of students and the renovation of his nature is his rescue from the fearful subjection to sense which is his ordinary state.

It should be noted that critical thinking is largely done in reaction to things we read, so the student with a civilian background might, upon reading this sentence, first feel that he or she has to "translate" the wording to understand the content before reacting to the content. But if the student feels he or she has to do this several times, the student will likely conclude that the effort isn't worth the insights to be gained.

Even if students don't think that college is meant to change their intellectual understanding of things, most do assume that college will improve their critical thinking skills. But I would note that (1) critical thinking is done within a verbal context and often in reaction to a verbal entity, whether written or spoken; and (2) the student was introduced to the basic tools of critical thinking while in childhood.

Again, we are faced with the fact that when children are introduced to the tools of critical thinking, they cannot understand these tools or use them at the adult level. And it would appear that adults won't get to the adult level of understanding of critical thinking tools unless they see that they bring into college the childhood-level understanding and mastery of the tools of critical thinking and recognize the need to progress to a higher (and more differentiated) level. Indeed, it is a reasonably safe conjecture that students unavoidably bring a child's level of understanding of all things into their early adult years, and into college.

Thus, this chapter presents a system for reading academic texts that should help students shift from this childhood-level understanding of academic texts to the adult level. I want to emphasize that this procedure is *not* intended to make students produce academic writing, but it gives them tools so that they can always find a way to unpack dense academic writing.

College-Level Reading: The Skimming Process

College courses require a lot of reading, and students have a limited amount of time to read these texts. The temptation is to read a text slowly when it is difficult or dry, but this strategy usually leads to students falling behind in their reading. The skimming strategy can help you at least know the "lay of the land" in a text and its key "landmarks," or claims. The skimming method provides a way to read short assignments, such as a textbook chapter, as well as for entire books, a strategy that is helpful for research papers. The process for shorter-length texts is presented first.

READING METHOD for Essays and Textbook Chapters: Core Elements with ANALYSIS CONCERNS

I. First reading: Skim to get a feel for the **general trajectory** of the text—a sense of its parts and the length of each part. Aim for gaining a sense of the essay's whole structure.

a. Skim over the text lightly.

    1. **Find transitional words that mark the start of a new section.**

    2. Note repetitions of key words that mark section changes.

    3. These repeated words are also key ideas in the text.

b. Determine the major sections of the body of the essay/chapter.

    1. Note whether the title gives a focus to the text.

    2. Determine when the opening ends.

    3. Determine when the closing starts.

    4. Realize that the closing often echoes the opening.

    5. Determine how many paragraphs are devoted to each point.

II. **Second reading: Do a slower reading,** but perhaps not a close reading.

a. At this point, **identify more of the content**, the specific arguments or illustrations used to convey the writer's ideas.

b. A key analytical concept is to look for **contrasts,** for opposites being explored. For example:

    1. The author might be in favor of one side.

    2. Or, the author might be trying to show the positives of both sides.

    3. Sometimes the contrasts aren't opposites but distinctions that clarify the reader's understanding of the issue.

c. Note the kinds of evidence used in each body paragraph that support the argument or point of that paragraph.

    1. Does the author rely on personal observation?

    2. Does the author use expert opinion?

    3. Does the author use empirical studies or humanities scholarship?

    4. Does the author use evidence from popular culture?

    5. Does rhetorical wordplay help drive a point home?

d. When you come across a section that's hard to understand, skip it and continue on.

    1. Once you have a sense of the whole and its parts, return to that dense passage and see if it is any clearer.

    2. If not, the problem could be in you—perhaps you don't know the correct definition of a key term used in the text, for example.

    3. Or, it could **just as likely** be that the passage isn't written very well.

e. To unpack bad writing, use the Principles of Reader Expectations (PRE) as a diagnostic tool and as a device to revise the passage so that you can decipher its meaning (see chapter 5 for a full explanation of PRE).

III. **Third reading:** Examine the **functions of words** in each sentence and how a word relates to other words in the sentence. You identify the functions of words by using **PRE:**

a. Identify whether the verb voice is active or passive. Vague writing often uses the passive voice too often and unnecessarily.

b. Identify whether the subjects of verbs are persons or nominalizations. Nominalizations (nouns that are derived from verbs) often result in vague writing, especially when used in the subject position.

c. Identify whether familiar information begins sentences.

d. Identify the contract of each paragraph and determine if the sentences following it observe the contract.

To sum up, the following are attitudes that experienced readers bring to a text:

1. Reading is a dynamic activity—you must reread to really understand the text.

2. You can't expect the first reading to be that deep—skim first; let things jump out at you. Those are the ideas you need to know first. Build the next reading session on those ideas.

3. Expect your understanding of the text to change, deepen with each rereading.

READING METHOD for Skimming Books

There are a variety of ways to read academic-level books, and most colleges have student services to help you achieve mastery of college-level material. What I provide here is a way to ensure that key words have at least been impressed into the soils of your mind, so that you can return to them later to bring out more connections. The following reading process will allow you to get a good sense of what is in the book in 15 minutes.

I. First, examine the **table of contents (TOC)**.

a. The table of contents is an outline of the book.

b. It will give you a sense of the key themes or topics that are covered in the book.

c. It is like the mental structure in the mind of the writer.

d. As a reader, you can imagine that you are installing that outline, that structure of understanding, into your own mind.

e. Also, as you dip into the book, you might want to refer back to the TOC to see where the content you have read fits in the overall scheme of the book.

II. Second, look in the **index** in the back of the book.

a. Skim the index for the key words you have identified.

b. Be aware that you might come across synonyms for the key words you are looking for.

c. Also see what words or names are used a lot in the book.
  1. You can detect how often a topic is mentioned by the number of page numbers after each term in the index.
  2. The more numbers, the more discussion is given to that topic.

III. Third, dip into the book by using key words from the index.

a. You could also dip into the book by using key words from the TOC.

b. Skim those few pages noted in the index to get a sense of writing style and perhaps some content.

IV. Fourth, read the **introduction**.

a. The introduction is often the last part of the text the author writes, but it is placed first in the book.

b. Here, the author sums up the book's thesis and arguments.

c. Often you'll find summaries of each of the chapters.

d. You'll also find explanations of the author's purpose and perhaps notice any biases the author might have.

Don't do this overview too quickly, but limit yourself to 15 minutes for each book. By then you should have a sense of what is in the book, enough to write an annotation. Also, as you notice that scholars use many of the same historical documents and agreed-upon concepts, you will become familiar with the issues these deal with. You'll notice what concepts are backed with scholarly consensus and which concepts are still being debated.

Tutorial: Getting the Student (Joe and Jane Civilian) to Read Academic Texts

Academic texts can be difficult for first-year college students to read for many reasons, and one of these reasons is that students have (without knowing this) expectations about the structures of sentences that are different from those of the academic text, especially in terms of the identities of subjects and verbs. For this reason, I present the following tutorial on how to get through difficult academic text passages.

A key thing to keep in mind as you read these sentences by Joe Academy is that although they are at first hard to read, they are grammatically correct, which means you can find subjects and verbs in them. So, look for verbs first and then subjects, which will be in front of the main verbs. As you do that, you are beginning to digest—in an indirect way—the content of the text. After some subject–verb practice, I'll show you a few other ways to "translate" academic texts so that you can even master the most difficult ones.

Throughout, after an example text, I will set passage sentences flush left to highlight or underscore the distance of the verb (V) from the subject (S), and then show how that feature causes difficulty, which is then compounded by identity surprises.

Here is an **abstract** from an academic text. The academic "abstract" is a specialized kind of writing and uses passive-voice verbs and non-person subjects as a way to be direct about the content of the article. Notice that the passage meets the academic PRE for subject–verb identities.

In the past decade transfer has seen a resurgence of attention in an effort to clarify some of its more difficult characteristics. One characteristic that requires a better description in the transfer literature is far transfer. The distance of transfer is often a very subjective matter depending on how similar the base and target are proposed to be. Four levels at which relations of similarity can be made are outlined in an effort to better describe judgments on transfer distance. Each increased level corresponds to a more distant form of transfer with far transfer occurring when judgments at the highest level of similarity are used. This highest level of similarity is called thematic similarity. Similarity at the thematic level is distinguished from the previous three levels in that judgments at this level are prefigurative rather than structural. Far transfer is formally defined to occur when themes are the primary source of similarity between a target and base and when the structure of the problem is ill-defined from the actor's perspective. Due to the often tacit nature of prefigurative themes, high priority is given in discussing the testability of these ideas.

Source: Forsyth, B. R. (2009, July). Defining far transfer via thematic similarity. Poster presented at the Annual Meeting of the 31st Annual Conference of the Cognitive Science Society, Amsterdam, The Netherlands.

Now, here is the same passage with flush-left diagramming (FLD) that highlights the subject and verb identities as they are preferred by the academic (see chapter 6 for a full explanation of flush left diagramming).

Note the following symbols used in the annotated passage:

→: this means that the action verb is an active-voice verb (AVV)

←: this means that the action verb is a passive-voice verb (PVV)

=: this means that the verb should be called an "equal sign verb;" that is —
the verb conveys no action, and the wording following the equal sign
verb describes features of the grammatical subject.

In the past decade
transfer has seen →
a resurgence of attention in an effort to clarify some of its more difficult
characteristics.
One characteristic that requires a better description in the transfer literature is =
far transfer.
The
distance of transfer is =
often a very subjective matter depending on how similar the
base and target are proposed ←
to be.
Four levels at which relations of similarity can be made are outlined ←
in an effort to better describe judgments on transfer distance.
Each increased level corresponds →
to a more distant form of transfer with far transfer occurring when
judgments at the highest level of similarity are used. ←
This highest level of similarity is called ←
thematic similarity.
Similarity at the thematic level is distinguished ←
from the previous three levels in that
judgments at this level are =
prefigurative rather than structural.
Far transfer is formally defined ←
to occur when
themes are =
the primary source of similarity between a target and base and when the
structure of the problem is ill-defined ←
from the actor's perspective.
Due to the often tacit nature of prefigurative themes, high
priority is given ←
in discussing the testability of these ideas.

QUANTIFICATION:
# of words: 190
# of SV combos: 14 (Count the number of flush-left lines.)
# of people S: 0
of "thing" S: 14
of pronoun S: 0
# of AVV: 2 (Indicated by the → arrow.)
# of PVV: 8 (Indicated by the ← arrow.)
# of equal sign verbs: 4 (Indicated by the = sign.)

COMMENTS: Just by looking at the identities of subjects and verbs (i.e., 14 "thing" subjects), it's clear why students might have some initial difficulty in getting their intellectual teeth into this text. Granted, it is an abstract, but all abstracts have this compression of verbalization, which uses lots of PVV (when the actor of the action isn't of a concern to the community of readers) and non-person subjects, and abstracts are something students continually encounter in their college years.

Despite this initial difficulty, if you have the vocabulary of PRE, you can skim paragraphs such as these, looking to see whether the first SV combo occurs early in each sentence and whether the subject is a person or a thing. If you are aware that academics prefer non-people subjects in some parts of their academic texts (because it puts the focus on the action rather than the actor), and that the non-people noun could be a nominalization, you will be able to skim such passages and, if not digest the content of the text, at least perceive what words are causing a lack of ingestion and digestion. If you have not yet reached that level of enlightened adult understanding of words and engagement with words, it helps to set the sentences flush left as in the example passage.

Let's look at another example using the same format for analysis. First is the original paragraph from a philosophy text by Prof. Catherine Leyshon, followed by the same paragraph with flush-left formatting, and then quantification and comments, as in the previous example.

The commitment to research that is relevant and interesting for lots of people and not just the scholarly community has changed the lifecycle of ideas. In the past this lifecycle might have been characterized by research which was developed in an academic department and disseminated to other academics through conferences and scholarly publications. It is easy to imagine that academics have the monopoly on producing ideas for research that are funded by organizations like the Arts & Humanities Research Council. But shifts in the way that research funding is distributed and accounted for have rightly encouraged a change in this lifecycle. It is increasingly the case that ideas are developed collaboratively in partnership between universities, voluntary organizations, charitable trusts, government and businesses. If the stuff of arts and humanities research can be found in every aspect of everyday life, as I argue above, it would be counter-intuitive for ideas to emerge only from one group of people working in universities and for the results to be useful only to academic audiences.

The
commitment to research that is relevant and interesting for lots of people and not
just the
scholarly
community
has changed
the lifecycle of ideas.
In the past
this lifecycle might have been characterized
by research
which was developed
in an academic department and
[which was] disseminated
to other academics through conferences and scholarly publications.
It is
easy to imagine that
academics have
the monopoly on producing ideas for research
that are funded
by organizations like the Arts & Humanities Research Council.
But
shifts in the way that research funding is distributed and accounted for have
rightly encouraged
a change in this lifecycle.
It is
increasingly the case that
ideas are developed

collaboratively in partnership between universities, voluntary organizations, charitable trusts, government and businesses.

If the

stuff of arts and humanities research can be found

in every aspect of everyday life, as

I argue

above,

it would be

counter-intuitive for ideas to emerge only from one group of people working in universities and for the results to be useful only to academic audiences.

QUANTIFICATION:

# of SV combos: 13

# of people S: 2

of "thing" S: 4

of pronoun S: 7

# of AVV: 4

# of PVV: 6

# of equal sign verbs: 3

COMMENTS: A remarkable feature of this paragraph is how far the first main verb is from its subject—and the subject is a nominalization. There is one secondary SV in that flush-left line. More than likely, the text wasn't too difficult for you to comprehend, even with so few people subjects. Almost all of the actions referred to are actions done by adults; it is interesting to consider how the text would sound if all of the PVVs were changed into AVVs, which would require the creation of actor-subjects—that is, people. In fact, you will do just that in one of the activities at the end of this chapter. SV combos of that caliber would trigger more vivid and specific images than the abstract nouns that presently inhabit the subject position.

Again, the intent here isn't to say that this is bad writing—it is to explain why the first-year college student might find this difficult, and to illustrate the techniques that make it easier to understand.

Introduction to the Reader Section

Below are four essays, with two assignments connected to each reading. A writing assignment is explained at the end of each essay and a Tear Out Sheet (TOS) is also assigned. The assignments help the student to identify the major aspects in each essay and to see some of the structural elements of the essay as well.

Stafford Essay

This essay deals with attitudes that a student should have when beginning a writing project, but it fits well with our discussion of college reading methods. As you read, I'd like you to be aware of the contrasts that the author sets up throughout the essay. After you read the essay a couple times, be sure to identify some of the contrasts that he proposes. I'll give you a hint about the first one: it is in the first sentence. You don't have to mention the other contrasts in your writing assignment (that deals with a different task), but we will discuss the content in terms of contrasts in class.

Writing Assignment

Write a 500 word response to this question about Stafford's essay: What does he say in the essay that surprises you, and why, and what does he say that you are already familiar with. **NOTE: Use MLA citation format.** Include three quotations and place the tagline in three different places (that is, place a tagline before a quotation, one within the quotation and one after the quotation). Include a bibliography, treating the essay as a work in an anthology. See the chapter on Research Mechanics for an example.

In addition, complete the TOS on page 91 in this chapter.

Writing
William Stafford

William Stafford (1914–1993) grew up in Kansas and taught at Lewis and Clark College in Oregon. His books include Traveling Through the Dark (1963), which received the National Book Award; Stories That Could Be True (1977), a collection of poems; Writing the Australian Crawl (1978), a collection of essays; A Glass Face in the Rain (1982); You Must Revise Your Life (1986), another collection of essays; An Oregon Message (1987); and Passwords (1991). Stafford describes a writing process that works for him—and might for you—in this timeless 1970 essay.

A writer is not so much someone who has something to say as he is someone who has found a process that will bring about new things he would not have thought of if he had not started to say them. That is, he does not draw on a reservoir; instead, he engages in an activity that brings to him a whole succession of unforeseen stories, poems, essays, plays, laws, philosophies, religions, or—but wait!

Back in school, from the first when I began to try to write things, I felt this richness. One thing would lead to another; the world would give and give. Now, after twenty years or so of trying, I live by that certain richness, an idea hard to pin, difficult to say, and perhaps offensive to some. For there are strange implications in it.

One implication is the importance of just plain receptivity. When I write, I like to have an interval before me when I am not likely to be interrupted. For me, this means

Excerpted from "A Way of Writing.", *Field: Contemporary Poetry and Poetics*, no. 2. Published by Oberlin College Press.

usually the early morning, before others are awake. I get pen and paper, take a glance out the window (often it is dark out there), and wait. It is like fishing. But I do not wait very long, for there is always a nibble—and this is where receptivity comes in. To get started I will accept anything that occurs to me. Something always occurs, of course, to any of us. We can't keep from thinking. Maybe I have to settle for an immediate impression: it's cold, or hot, or dark, or bright, or in between! Or—well, the possibilities are endless. If I put down something, that thing will help the next thing come, and I'm off. If I let the process go on, things will occur to me that were not at all in my mind when I started. These things, odd and trivial as they may be, are somehow connected. And if I let them string out, surprising things will happen.

If I let them string out ... Along with initial receptivity, then, there is another readiness: I must be willing to fail. If I am to keep on writing, I cannot bother to insist on high standards. I must get into action and not let anything stop me, or even slow me much. By "standards" I do not mean "correctness"—spelling, punctuation, and so on. These details become mechanical for anyone who writes for a while. I am thinking about what many people would consider "important" standards, such matters as social significance, positive values, consistency, etc. I resolutely disregard these. Something better, greater, is happening! I am following a process that leads so wildly and originally into new territory that no judgment can at the moment be made about values, significance, and so on. I am making something new, something that has not been judged before. Later others—and maybe I myself—will make judgments. Now, I am headlong to discover. Any distraction may harm the creating.

So, receptive, careless of failure, I spin out things on the page. And a wonderful freedom comes. If something occurs to me, it is all right to accept it. It has one justification: it occurs to me. No one else can guide me. I must follow my own weak, wandering, diffident impulses.

A strange bonus happens. At times, without my insisting on it, my writings become coherent; the successive elements that occur to me are clearly related. They lead by themselves to new connections. Sometimes the language, even the syllables that happen along, may start a trend. Sometimes the materials alert me to something waiting in my mind, ready for sustained attention. At such times, I allow myself to be eloquent, or intentional, or for great swoops (treacherous! not to be trusted!) reasonable. But I do not insist on any of that; for I know that back of my activity there will be the coherence of my self, and that indulgence of my impulses will bring recurrent patterns and meanings again.

This attitude toward the process of writing creatively suggests a problem for me, in terms of what others say. They talk about "skills" in writing. Without denying that I do have experience, wide reading, automatic orthodoxies and maneuvers of various kinds, I still must insist that I am often baffled about what "skill" has to do with the precious little area of confusion when I do not know what I am going to say and then I found out what I am going to say. That precious interval I am unable to bridge by skill. What can I witness about it? It remains mysterious, just as all of us must feel puzzled about how we are so inventive as to be able to talk along through complexities with our friends, not needing to plan what we are going to say, but never stalled for long in our confident forward progress. Skill? If so, it is the skill we all have, something we must have learned before the age of three or four.

A writer is one who has become accustomed to trusting that grace, or luck, or—skill.

Yet another attitude I find necessary: most of what I write, like most of what I say in casual conversation, will not amount to much. Even I will realize, and even at the time, that it is not negotiable. It will be like practice. In conversation, I allow myself random remarks—in fact, as I recall, that is the way I learned to talk—so in writing I launch many expendable efforts. A result of this free way of writing is that I am not writing for others, mostly; they will not see the product at all unless the activity eventuates in something that later appears to be worthy. My guide is the self, and its adventuring in the language brings about communication.

This process-rather-than-substance view of writing invites a final, dual reflection:

1. Writers may not be special—sensitive or talented in any usual sense. They are simply engaged in sustained use of a language skill we all have. Their "creations" come about through confident reliance on stray impulses that will, with trust, find occasional patterns that are satisfying.

2. But writing itself is one of the great, free human activities. There is scope for individuality, and elation, and discovery, in writing. For the person who follows with trust and forgiveness what occurs to him, the world remains always ready and deep, an inexhaustible environment, with the combined vividness of an actuality and flexibility of a dream. Working back and forth between experience and thought, writers have more than space and time can offer. They have the whole unexplored realm of human vision.

Sanders Essay

As you read this essay, notice the expectations generated in your mind by his title, and then by the first paragraph of the essay. At the end of the essay, write some notes (not to be handed in) about how you could convert the title into a complete sentence that expresses his thesis. Also bring some ideas to class about the relationship of the first paragraph to the rest of the essay.

Sanders Essay

As you read this essay, notice the expectations generated in your mind by the title, and then by the first paragraph of the essay. At the end of the essay, write some notes (not to be handed in) about how you could convert the title into a complete sentence that expresses the author's thesis. Also, bring some ideas to class about the relationship of the first paragraph to the rest of the essay.

Writing Assignment

Pick three sentences from the Sanders essay and explain how he either meets or violates the expectations that the civilian reader has about location and identities of subject and their verbs. Provide a flush left diagram of each sentence before you describe the sentence's features. Include a bibliography, treating the essay as a work in an anthology. See the chapter on Research Mechanics for an example.

In addition, complete the worksheet on p 93 in this chapter.

The Men We Carry in Our Minds

Scott Russell Sanders

Scott Russell Sanders (1945–) was born in Memphis, Tennessee, attended Brown University and took a Ph.D. at Cambridge University. He writes on a variety of subjects for "little" magazines such as The Georgia Review and The North American Review and for more commercial publications such as Omni and Isaac Asimov's Science Fiction Magazine. His published books include Wonder's Hidden: Audubon's Early Years (1984), Hear the Wind Blow: American Folksongs Retold (1985), and The Paradise of Bombs (1987). His writing is characteristically rich in detail and focused on the ironies and complexities of human experience. In this essay on memories of men, written in 1984, Sanders takes exception to certain assumptions of modern feminism.

The first men, besides my father, I remember seeing were black convicts and white guards, in the cotton field across the road from our farm on the outskirts of Memphis. I must have been three or four. The prisoners wore dingy gray-and-black zebra suits, heavy as canvas, sodden with sweat. Hatless, stooped, they chopped weeds in the fierce heat, row after row, breathing the acrid dust of boll-weevil poison. The overseers wore dazzling white shirts and broad shadowy hats. The oiled barrels of their shotguns flashed in the sunlight. Their faces in memory are utterly blank. Of course those men, white and black, have become for me an emblem of racial hatred. But they have also come to stand for the twin poles of my early vision of manhood—the brute toiling animal and the boss.

When I was a boy, the men I knew labored with their bodies. They were marginal farmers, just scraping by, or welders, steelworkers, carpenters; they swept floors, dug ditches, mined coal, or drove trucks, their forearms ropy with muscle; they trained horses, stoked furnaces, built tires, stood on assembly lines wrestling parts onto cars and refrigerators. They got up before light, worked all day long whatever the weather, and when they came home at night they looked as though somebody had been whipping them. In the evenings and on weekends they worked on their own places, tilling gardens that were lumpy with clay, fixing broken-down cars, hammering on houses that were always too drafty, too leaky, too small.

The bodies of the men I knew were twisted and maimed in ways visible and invisible. The nails of their hands were black and split, the hands tattooed with scars. Some had lost fingers. Heavy lifting had given many of them finicky backs and guts weak from hernias. Racing against conveyor belts had given them ulcers. Their ankles and knees ached from years of standing on concrete. Anyone who had worked for long around machines was hard of hearing. They squinted, and the skin of their faces was creased like the leather of old work gloves. There were times, studying them, when I dreaded growing up. Most of them coughed, from dust or cigarettes, and most of them drank cheap wine or whisky, so their eyes looked bloodshot and bruised. The fathers of my friends always seemed older than the mothers. Men wore out sooner. Only women lived into old age.

As a boy I also knew another sort of men, who did not sweat and break down like mules. They were soldiers, and so far as I could tell they scarcely worked at all. During my early school years we lived on a military base, an arsenal in Ohio, and every day I saw GIs in the guard shacks, on the stoops of barracks, at the wheels of olive drab Chevrolets. The chief fact of their lives was boredom. Long after I left the Arsenal I came to recognize the sour smell the soldiers gave off as that of souls in limbo. They were all waiting—for wars, for transfers, for leaves, for promotions, for the end of their hitch—like so many braves waiting for the hunt to begin. Unlike the warriors of older tribes, however, they would have no say about when the battle would start or how it would be waged. Their waiting was broken only when they practiced for war. They fired guns at targets, drove tanks across the churned-up fields of the military reservation, set off bombs in the wrecks of old fighter planes. I knew this was all play. But I also felt certain that when the hour for killing arrived, they would kill. When the real shooting started, many of them would die. This was what soldiers were *for*, just as a hammer was for driving nails.

Warriors and toilers: those seemed, in my boyhood vision, to be the chief destinies for men. They weren't the only destinies, as I learned from having a few male teachers, from reading books, and from watching television. But the men on television—the politicians, the astronauts, the generals, the savvy lawyers, the philosophical doctors, the bosses who gave orders to both soldiers and laborers—seemed as removed and unreal to me as the figures in tapestries. I could no more imagine growing up to become one of these cool, potent creatures than I could imagine becoming a prince.

A nearer and more hopeful example was that of my father, who had escaped from a red-dirt farm to a tire factory, and from the assembly line to the front office. Eventually he dressed in a white shirt and tie. He carried himself as if he had been born to work with his mind. But his body, remembering the earlier years of slogging work, began to give out on him in his fifties, and it quit on him entirely before he turned sixty-five. Even such a partial escape from man's fate as he had accomplished did not seem possible for most of the boys I knew. They joined the Army, stood in line for jobs in the smoky plants, helped build highways. They were bound to work as their fathers had worked, killing themselves or preparing to kill others.

A scholarship enabled me not only to attend college, a rare enough feat in my circle, but even to study in a university meant for the children of the rich. Here I met for the first time young men who had assumed from birth that they would lead lives of comfort and power. And for the first time I met women who told me that men were guilty of having kept all the joys and privileges of the earth for themselves. I was baffled. What privileges? What joys? I thought about the maimed, dismal lives of most of the men back home. What had they stolen from their wives and daughters? The right to go five days a week, twelve months a year, for thirty or forty years to a steel mill or a coal mine? The right to drop bombs and die in war? The right to feel every leak in the roof, every gap in the fence, every cough in the engine, as a wound they must mend? The right to feel, when the lay-off comes or the plant shuts down, not only afraid but ashamed?

I was slow to understand the deep grievances of women. This was because, as a boy, I had envied them. Before college, the only people I had ever known who were interested in art or music or literature, the only ones who read books, the only ones who ever seemed to enjoy a sense of ease and grace were the mothers and daughters. Like the men-folk, they fretted about money, they scrimped and made-do. But, when they pay stopped coming in, they were not the ones who had failed. Nor did they have to go to war, and that seemed to me a blessed fact. By comparison with the narrow, ironclad days of fathers, there was an expansiveness, I thought, in the days of mothers. They went to see neighbors, to shop in town, to run errands at school, at the library, at church. No doubt, had I looked harder at their lives, I would have envied them less. It was not my fate to become a woman, so it was easier for me to see the graces. Few of them held jobs outside the home, and those who did filled thankless roles as clerks and waitresses. I didn't see, then, what a prison a house could be, since houses seemed to me brighter, handsomer places than any factory. I did not realize—because such things were never spoken of—how often women suffered from men's bullying. I did learn about the wretchedness of abandoned wives, single mothers, widows; but I also learned about the wretchedness of lone men. Even then I could see how exhausting it was for a mother to cater all day to the needs of young children. But if I had been asked, as a boy, to choose between tending a baby and tending a machine, I think I would have chosen the baby. (Having now tended both, I know I would choose the baby.)

So I was baffled when the women at college accused me and my sex of having cornered the world's pleasures. I think something like my bafflement has been felt by other boys (and girls as well) who grew up in dirt-poor farm country, in mining country, in black ghettos, in Hispanic barrios, in the shadows of factories, in Third World nations—any place where the fate of men is as grim and bleak as the fate of women. Toilers and warriors. I realize now how ancient these identities are, how deep the tug they exert on men, the undertow of a thousand generations. The miseries I saw, as a boy, in the lives of nearly all men I continue to see in the lives of many—the body-breaking toil, the tedium, the call to be tough, the humiliating powerlessness, the battle for a living and for territory.

When the women I met at college thought about the joys and privileges of men, they did not carry in their minds the sort of men I had known in my childhood. They thought of their fathers, who were bankers, physicians, architects, stockbrokers, the big wheels of the big cities. These fathers rode the train to work or drove cars that cost more than any of my childhood houses. They were attended from morning to night by female helpers, wives and nurses and secretaries. They were never laid off, never short of cash at month's end, never lined up for welfare. These fathers made decisions that mattered. They ran the world.

The daughters of such men wanted to share in this power, this glory. So did I. They yearned for a say over their future, for jobs worthy of their abilities, for the right to live at peace, unmolested, whole. Yes, I thought, yes yes. The difference between me and these daughters was that they saw me, because of my sex, as destined from birth to become like their fathers, and therefore as an enemy to their desires. I was an ally. If I had known, then, how to tell them so, would they have believed me? Would they now?

Frye Essay

Frye speaks of students coming into college with assumptions that are at odds with what faculty assume. He writes about what constitutes thinking and thought-filled expression, and he points out some of the sad ironies that we in a free society live with in regard to words and thinking. As you read this, notice the ways this text is attempting to do what he feels is needed (although my scheme didn't rise directly from this essay!).

Writing Assignment

Explain Frye's ideas on what it means to be a thinking person. Use three quotations from his essay, and place taglines in three different locations. Also include in your essay ways in which Frye's essay reflects your experience (good and bad) with words. Final draft length: 450–550 words. Include a bibliography, treating the essay as a work in an anthology.

In addition, complete the TOS on page 95 in this chapter

Don't You Think It's Time to Start Thinking?

Northrop Frye

Northrop Frye (1912–1991), one of Canada's most distinguished scholars, was reared in New Brunswick, and after attending school in Canada, received his MA from Oxford University, in England (1940). In 1939 Frye became a professor at the University of Toronto, where he wrote and taught until his death. His interests were literary criticism and school curriculum; his books include On Education *and* Myth and Metaphor. *The following essay insists that thinking happens only when a person writes down ideas "in the right words."*

A student often leaves high school today without any sense of language as a structure.

He may also have the idea that reading and writing are elementary skills that he mastered in childhood, never having grasped the fact that there are differences in levels of reading and writing as there are in mathematics between short division and integral calculus.

Yet, in spite of his limited verbal skills, he firmly believes that he can think, that he has ideas, and that if he is just given the opportunity to express them he will be all right. Of course, when you look at what he's written you find it doesn't make any sense. When you tell him this he is devastated.

Part of his confusion here stems from the fact that we use the word "think" in so many bad, punning ways. Remember James Thurber's Walter Mitty who was always dreaming great dreams of glory. When his wife asked him what he was doing he would say, "Has it ever occurred to you that I might be thinking?"

But, of course, he wasn't thinking at all. Because we use it for everything our minds do, worrying, remembering, daydreaming, we imagine that thinking is something that can be achieved without any training. But again it's a matter of practice. How well we can think depends on how much of it we have already done. Most students need to be taught, very carefully and patiently, that there is no such thing as an inarticulate idea waiting to have the right words wrapped around it.

They have to learn that ideas do not exist until they have been incorporated into words. Until that point you don't know whether you are pregnant or just have gas on the stomach.

The operation of thinking is the practice of articulating ideas until they are in the right words. And we can't think at random either. We can only add one more idea to the body of something we have already thought about. Most of us spend very little time doing this, and that is why there are so few people whom we regard as having any power to articulate at all. When such a person appears in public life, like Mr. Trudeau, we tend to regard him as possessing a gigantic intellect.

A society like ours doesn't have very much interest in literacy. It is compulsory to read and write because society must have docile and obedient citizens. We are taught to read so that we can obey the traffic signs and to cipher so that we can make out our income tax, but development of verbal competency is very much left to the individual.

And when we look at our day-to-day existence we can see that there are strong currents at work against the development of powers of articulateness. Young adolescents today often betray a curious sense of shame about speaking articulately, of framing a sentence with a period at the end of it.

Part of the reason for this is the powerful anti-intellectual drive which is constantly present in our society. Articulate speech marks you out as an individual, and in some settings this can be rather dangerous because people are often suspicious and frightened of articulateness. So if you say as little as possible and use only stereotyped, ready-made phrases you can hide yourself in the mass.

Then there are various epidemics sweeping over society which use unintelligibility as a weapon to preserve the present power structure. By making things as unintelligible as possible, to as many people as possible, you can hold the present power structure together. Understanding and articulateness lead to its destruction. This is the kind of thing that George Orwell was talking about, not just in *Nineteen Eighty-Four*, but in all his work on language. The kernel of everything reactionary and tyrannical in society is the impoverishment of the means of verbal communication.

The vast majority of things that we hear today are prejudices and clichés, simply verbal formulas that have no thought behind them but are put up as pretence of thinking. It is not until we realize these things conceal meaning, rather than reveal it, that we can begin to develop our own powers of articulateness.

The teaching of humanities is, therefore, a militant job. Teachers are faced not simply with a mass of misconceptions and unexamined assumptions. They must engage in a fight to help the student confront and reject the verbal formulas and stock responses, to convert passive acceptance into active, constructive power. It is a fight against illiteracy and for the maturation of the mental process, for the development of skills which once acquired will never become obsolete.

Koch Essay

This essay was published in the online journal *Universitas* and it is included here to give you an example of the citation mechanics used in MLA format. In addition, it can be analyzed for its content, as it deals with the nature and purpose of liberal education.

Writing Assignment

Produce a 500 word final draft in which you explain how the ideas presented in this essay might affect your study habits and approach to your courses (not just this semester but in future semesters and when you are studying your major) as well as your understanding of college education. Use three quotes from the essay and place the tagline in three different places (that is, place a tagline before a quotation, one within the quotation and one after the quotation). Include a bibliography, treating the essay as a work in an anthology. See the chapter on Research Mechanics for an example.

In addition, complete the TOS on page 97 in this chapter.

Liberal Education for a Time of Uncertainty: Reflections on Mark Van Doren's *Liberal Education*

Bill Koch

For several months now I have been reading up on composition theory, and I've noticed that scholars like Anne Berthoff and Patricia Bizzell quote some of the seminal thinkers and philosophers of the early 20th century. These scholars (such as Cassirer, Richards, Whitehead) wrote their most influential texts during the 1930s, as if the awful gathering military storm had pressured these thinkers into formulating crystalline expressions of what the human mind must do to—as Richards puts it—"remedy our misunderstandings" (12).

We live in a time of a gathering storm, too, if not in the storm itself. And another writer who might help us during our troubling times is Mark Van Doren, who wrote and published *Liberal Education* in 1943, and we all know what was going on then.

But I propose commenting on this book for another reason too: the University of Northern Iowa has begun to formally examining its Liberal Arts Core, and I find that Van Doren says many things relevant to our mission as a Liberal Arts institution.

Van Doren felt the topic was important enough to broach even in the midst of a world wide conflagration; indeed, he felt this war demanded that academics rethink their mission so that the psychical pieces which remained after the war could be reconstructed with a modicum of tragic wisdom. Our times seem to be beckoning us to do the same. How can academia contribute to a global educational program that meets the needs (physical and psychical) of humanity while also respecting the prerogatives of specific nations? How can academia—perhaps more accurately, how can liberal education—most effectively shape students so they will and can contribute to the fruition of humanity's potential and dreams? This is another way of saying—how can Liberal Education help students fulfill their destiny?

I find it interesting that in the Preface for the 1959 edition of *Liberal Education*, Van Doren notes that scientists doubt their own wisdom, and that the layman feels he has no capacity to wisely judge the merits of science. Yet, Van Doren declares, "This is the age of science: an age, oddly enough, in which it might be said that we know less than ever before what we are doing." Hence, "the age of science is [...] also [...] an age of ignorance" (n.p.).

Thus Van Doren presents the irony that because we doubt our wisdom, because ignorance pervades this age of science and experts, it is clear that **"there is a great deal to be thought about [and] as many persons as possible should do the thinking"** (n.p.). [As to what exactly constitutes thinking will be a topic Van Doren discusses in his book.]

For Van Doren, liberal education lives up to its ideal when opinion "flourishes and argument goes on: **argument, that is to say, about the greatest things, the difficult, the all but insoluble things that haunt us every morning as we wake."**

Van Doren notes that a Liberal Arts Education (LAE) is not an end in itself. Rather, "it prepares the intellect to search for [answers to tough questions] and to recognize [them] when or if [they are] available" (n.p.) This means that while course content (such as the readings of a humanities course, the lab work of a science course) provides important knowledge, a LAE must insure that another type of knowledge is conveyed <u>through</u> content: "**knowledge of the intellect and its powers, [...] its powers of precision**" (n.p.).

I would posit that our present LAC framework needs to highlight this kind of knowledge and precision better, because precision deals with the processes of thinking that transcend all disciplines. And I would submit that precision development begins with the assumptions we have about the nature, power and limits of thinking.

When I begin my College Reading and Writing class I am always struck by the divergence between myself and the students over our assumptions about the nature of education and learning. You can't fault students too much for this, because their assumptions come from the larger society that convinces them that material things are most important, that a happy life is filled with things and activities, that an education's purpose is to improve one's chances of getting a "good" job. We as faculty must move students from these unhelpful assumptions to assumptions that affect their understanding of the nature of the intellect and its powers, assumptions that reveal to students how they can learn how to learn.

Van Doren identifies one of these faulty assumptions. Everyone knows that precision operates in science, he says, but "the student doubts it operates anywhere else. [...] But the precision of Shakespeare was marvelous, too, and of Mozart and of Dante" (n.p.**When Liberal Education shows the student that the precision of mind is possible on many "fronts**," then the student can learn to "be at home with the intellect at its happiest, even though most of its masters are dead" (n.p.)

When a student reads literary achievements, he or she is in "contact with the mind at its happiest, [which] makes the dead come alive," Van Doren says, and "to that extent, [the student's] own life increases, for he knows how to think of every great mind as his contemporary. He is prepared then to add to the whole glory if he can" (n.p.).

I find that last statement especially compelling, and a similar thought occurred to me this past semester. I tell my students that we require them to take courses in a variety of fields for two reasons: not just to expose them to the achievements (and failures) that contributed to our present situation, but—more importantly—to show students that those inventors and thinkers were human beings just like them. And I challenge them to believe that **their knowledge of the past should show them that they too could come up with the Next Big Idea**. Why not?

Van Doren's 1959 introduction reiterates his original conclusion of 1943 that Liberal Education "is a specific discipline, and has rules, also an inescapable content" (n.p.). He then dryly notes, "I am not aware that during the years since then there has been much agreement with this claim" (n.p.) But he was not advancing his own views on the discipline, just the claim "that the discipline exists [. . .and] that the chief duty of teachers is to discover its content" (n.p.).

I don't know if it's an irony or just interesting, but my own scholarship of the past year has suggested to me what that content might be, and I am now using Van Doren as a vehicle (and a crutch?) to outline—and test— this content, this discipline. And it is the genius of the discipline and content (but not of me) that if we are to fill in the outline of a LAE, the faculty (and students?) must discuss the issues, argue for their position, listen to each other, weigh the merits of various opinions, and try to come to a workable consensus. But I would also repeat the focus of our discussions. They should be about, as Van Doren says, "the greatest things, the difficult, the all but insoluble things."

In connection to this last point, Van Doren concludes his introduction with remarks that seem to be directed specifically to those of us on this campus:

> Any college can be better than it is; but all colleges would be better if those in charge of them considered together, at regular intervals, the ideal college curriculum. They would not need to fear that every college would then become identical with every other; such identities cannot exist in nature. But if all liberal colleges had the same aim, and if they were serious in their pursuit of it, the differences among them would become, for a change, really interesting. (n.p.)

Concerning that same aim, Van Doren writes, "I continue to believe that the way to produce individual intellects is **to teach** all students the **same things**, and of course the **best things**" (n.p.)

Van Doren's first chapter, "Nobody Thinks He is Educated," characterizes general features of a liberal education that I think most academics would agree with:

- "Education can afford to ponder **programs of being** no less deeply than schedules of doing" (5).
- A parent "is not told [but should be told?] to expect the transformation inside the son which tradition takes to be the main thing" (6).
- Students "can benefit by knowing that education is something they must labor to give themselves" (7).

- "The good educator is very **serious** but also very s**ensible**. And somewhere in his soul there is a **saving lightness**" (7).

- "The good educator knows that the secret of the discipline he imparts is not the final secret of existence. [...] **Education does not pose as insurance against error and sin**. [...] The world of men must manage itself. With education it can be wiser, but deeper things decide its fate" (8).

- "Modesty in an educator bases itself, furthermore, upon his perception that **accident plays a high role in the affairs of human life**, including the affairs of education" (9).

All of these remarks lay out the limits and the power of liberal education's mission, and when we perceive the limits of education, education "becomes truly important" (7).

In the same vein of humility, Van Doren declares that although he may be an expert on Shakespeare, "[this] book is not by one who considers himself educated. It is by one who still wishes to be, and who has set out to discover, if he can, of what the experience would consist" (11).

Van Doren identifies three things that an educated person must have "**a reasonably deep and clear feeling about** the bearings upon one another, and upon his own mind" (11). Those three things are, significantly I think, "**art, science and religion**." Van Doren claims that an educated person by definition necessarily "arrives at the center from which these radiate—if there is a center. He would like to know that first of all, and to realize what knowledge of it means" (11).

But he then notes that his own education has been mostly literary, while society as a whole values the sciences over the literary (and whatever is valued the most becomes that person's religion, it seem to me).

The implication, I think, is that an ideal (but eminently possible) liberal education provides equal doses of knowledge (which it presently provides adequately, though by itself is thin gruel), reflection (often lacking) and experience (including practicing an art–also often lacking).

Perhaps we could call those 3 "doses" the 3 prongs of methodology: knowledge of a topic, reflection on that topic, and experience in it (in lab and in studio).

(In addition, would the 3 prongs of content would be art, science and religion?)

Van Doren observes that this kind of bare outline says little about what a complete education, "within the limits of human reason and imagination," should result in (12). I would pose these as the outcomes:

First, **one develops a perpetual flexibility of intellectual cognitivity** (a neologism, I know) such that, to quote Robert Pirsig from his book *Zen and the Art of Motorcycle Maintenance*,

One's rational understanding [...] is modified [...] as one [...] sees that a new and different rational understanding has more Quality. One [won't] cling to old sticky ideas [when] one has an immediate rational basis for rejecting them. [... Then] you never get stuck. [Rationality] has forms but the forms are capable of change. (363-4)

As Van Doren will later declare in his book. "The liberal arts are the liberating arts" (79). I believe we should take those words seriously and see their radical implications.

Second, **one develops what Kieran Egan calls a philosophical and ironic level of understanding (PIU).** By philosophic he means that one has not only ingested a lot of information, but one has digested it in a way that helps him or her realize that one's prior understanding of a particular topic, or value one adheres to, was very partial, incomplete, and unable to handle the complexities of the modern world. And, I would suggest that when a student is aware of his or her level of understanding AND—more importantly— knows how to develop their understanding AND knows how to recognize humane development, then liberal education has fulfilled its mission.

In addition, with a PIU, one embraces an **ironic perspective**, too, the purpose of which is not to deflate values and ideals, but **to deflate one's hubris and egotism**, reminding one that no matter how sophisticated one's understanding has become through PIU, it is still provisional, likely to be reformed by the next day's news and discoveries. Irony reminds us that even education has its limits, and that life is bigger than our cognitive abilities.

So I would suggest that despite over 2,000 years of Western intellectual tradition, **we have barely gotten going in the education of the species**. (Lately I've suggested to students that we are just beginning to understand the power of literacy!) In fact, I'd say we are only **at the end of our childhood as a species**, though the signs can be interpreted as the End end. But I think such a view comes not from PIU but from an infantile, or adolescent mythic or romantic level of understanding.

Such levels of understanding have their value and purpose, and PIU itself has an element of the mythic and romantic (perhaps its saving graces—the "lightness" Van Doren referred to earlier). But an adult cannot consider himself or herself truly educated if he or she operates from a simplistic mythic or romantic perspective. That this is often the case is reflected in the axiom that newspapers try to write their news at a 6th grade level.

I would suggest then that **the time has come to articulate**, as a faculty, the **discipline of cognitivity that would transcend all disciplines**—this would be PIU?—and we have to hammer out its contents, a set of limited yet related ideas that all disciplines find useful, even necessary.

What that content might be may be is hinted at in Van Doren's next chapter, titled, "The Educated Person." My next essay (should anyone be interested) will discuss that chapter and perhaps more.

But as a closing image, I'd like to share a passage from the Jesuit scientist Teilhard de Chardin, who, even while being an ambulance carrier in World War I, found the optimism to write,

> So far a as one can guess, the developments [in biology] to be expected are primarily of the intellectual and moral order. The impression one gets is that after having been completely occupied for a long time in the work of constructing organisms**, life is only now beginning to see its internal dispositions**; it is concentrating its attention and care on advances and refinements of a finally **perfected consciousness**. At present, **evolution is continuing much more through improvements of the psychological order than through organic transformations**. (Writings in Time of War 17)

I would suggest that education, especially Liberal Education, now has the opportunity to unlock the doors of the psyche and activate the processes that refine biology's internal dispositions and advance them to levels we have not seen or expected, but should have.

It may seem the task has been going on a long time—a couple million years?—but perhaps PIU sees that as a very short period of time. The clay of consciousness has been built up; the first round of early urban civilizations has given the clay of consciousness its general features. Now may be the time to refine them—and fire them—in the furnace of self-examination and communal catharsis.

Works Cited or Authors Mentioned

Burke, Kenneth. The Philosophy of Literary Form. Berkeley: U of Calif Press, 1941

Egan, Kieran. The Educated Mind: How Cognitive Tools Shape our Understanding. Chicago: U of Chicago Press, 1997.

Casssirer, Ernst. An Essay on Man. New Haven: Yale, 1944.

Pirsig, Robert. Zen and the Art of Motorcycle Maintenance: An Inquiry Into Values. NY: Harper Torch, 2006 (1974).

Richards, I. A. How to Read a Page. New York: Norton, 1942.

Teilhard de Chardin, Pierre. Writings in Time of War. Trans. René Hague. 1st U.S. ed. New York: Harper and Row, 1968.

Whitehead, Alfred North. Adventures of Ideas. NY: MacMillan, 1933

Revision of Abstract

Return to the first example abstract on page 62 and change all the PVVs into AVVs.

PVV	AVV revision
1.	
2.	
3.	
4.	
5.	
6.	
7.	
8.	

# Revision of Abstract

NAME: .... CLASS HOUR: .... DATE: ....

Return to the abstract about commitment to research on page 64 and change all the PVVs into AVVs.

PVV	AVV revision
1.	
2.	
3.	
4.	
5.	
6.	

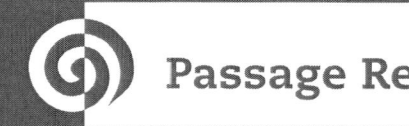

Passage Revision #1

Below is a passage from the Koch essay. Put V above the main Verbs and S above their subjects, then quantify the text using the list below. Then, on the reverse side of this page, flush left the passage. (As you flush left, you will need to use brackets to repeat a subject.)

      I don't know if it's an irony or just interesting, but my own scholarship of the past year has suggested to me what that content might be, and I am now using Van Doren as a vehicle (and a crutch?) to outline—and test—this content, this discipline. And it is the genius of the discipline and content (but not of me) that if we are to fill in the outline of a LAE, the faculty (and students?) must discuss the issues, argue for their position, listen to each other, weigh the merits of various opinions, and try to come to a workable consensus. But I would also repeat the focus of our discussions. They should be about, as Van Doren says, "the greatest things, the difficult, the all but insoluble things."

Quantify the text:

of words: 132

# of SV combos:

# of AVV:

# of PVV:

# of equal sign verbs:

# of people S:

of "thing" S:

of pronoun S:

Infinitives in sentence:

Nominalizations in sentence

Passage Revision #2

Below is a passage from the Koch essay. Put V above the main Verbs and S above their subjects, then quantify the text using the list below. Then, on the reverse side of this page, flush left the passage.

Any college can be better than it is; but all colleges would be better if those in charge of them considered together, at regular intervals, the ideal college curriculum. They would not need to fear that every college would then become identical with every other; such identities cannot exist in nature. But if all liberal colleges had the same aim, and if they were serious in their pursuit of it, the differences among them would become, for a change, really interesting.

Quantify the text:

of words: 81

# of SV combos:

# of AVV:

# of PVV:

# of equal sign verbs:

# of people S:

of "thing" S:

of pronoun S:

Infinitives in sentence:

Nominalizations in sentence:

Other remarks:

Convert these academic sentences into flush-left diagrams, and then circle words that convey action but aren't being used as verbs.

1. The new development of manufacture outside the guild system led to a vast increase in trade, to a new mobility of capital, to a new relationship between worker and employer.

2. Those who became eventually sensitized to the social pulse of their time found their way towards a sociological evaluation of their own position blocked by the proletariat.

3. To condense a bewildering volume of information to manageable proportions is to make available, sift and refine pertinent data for successive operations.

4. What makes Hegel's method of reasoning peculiar is his aim to reinterpret rather than to expand a given historical range of experience.

5. The analysis of the various strands of relativity is the analysis of the social structure of the Universe, as in this epoch.

6. Our perception of the geometrical order of the Universe brings with it the denial of the restrictions of inheritance to mere personal order.

7. I suggest that the development of systematic theology should be accompanied by a critical understanding of the relation of linguistic expression to our deepest and most persistent intuitions.

8. Despite these very serious drawbacks, I would like to try to retrieve the "cognitive process" of composing as an important site for deepening understanding about the nature of literacy.

9. Insights into the metacommunicative foundations of literacy help to resolve the paradox with which this study began, revealing social involvement as not merely a cultural impetus for literacy but its interpretive underpinning as well.

NAME: CLASS HOUR: DATE:

Identify the following in the Stafford essay.

1. Where does the start seem to end? easy to identify / hard to identify

2. Where does the end seem to start? easy to identify / hard to identify

3. What paragraphs appear to start with a transition?

4. How many paragraphs are present for each point?

5. What contrasts seem to be explicitly and implicitly stated?

6. What kinds of evidence seem preponderant?
    a. Personal observation
    b. Expert testimony
    c. Empirical studies
    d. Facts
    e. Other

7. Are any sections, paragraphs, or sentences hard to understand?

8. What metaphors are used?

NAME: .... CLASS HOUR: .... DATE: ....

Identify the following in the Sanders essay.

1. Where does the start seem to end? easy to identify / hard to identify

2. Where does the end seem to start? easy to identify / hard to identify

3. What paragraphs appear to start with a transition?

4. How many paragraphs are present for each point?

5. What contrasts seem to be explicitly and implicitly stated?

6. What kinds of evidence seem preponderant?
   a. Personal observation
   b. Expert testimony
   c. Empirical studies
   d. Facts
   e. Other

7. Are any sections, paragraphs, or sentences hard to understand?

8. What metaphors are used?

NAME: _____ CLASS HOUR: _____ DATE: _____

Identify the following in the Frye essay.

1. Where does the start seem to end? easy to identify / hard to identify

2. Where does the end seem to start? easy to identify / hard to identify

3. What paragraphs appear to start with a transition?

4. How many paragraphs are present for each point?

5. What contrasts seem to be explicitly and implicitly stated?

6. What kinds of evidence seem preponderant?
   a. Personal observation
   b. Expert testimony
   c. Empirical studies
   d. Facts
   e. Other

7. Are any sections, paragraphs, or sentences hard to understand?

8. What metaphors are used?

NAME: .... CLASS HOUR: .... DATE: ....

Below are the quotations from Mark Van Doren's book that were used in the Koch piece – rewrite each one so that a tagline is used, and put the tagline in different places, as instructed

1. "Education can afford to ponder **programs of being** no less deeply than schedules of doing" (5). (put the tagline before the quotation):

2. "The good educator is very **serious** but also very s**ensible**. And somewhere in his soul there is a **saving lightness**" (7). (put tagline within the quotation):

3. "The good educator knows that the secret of the discipline he imparts is not the final secret of existence" (8). (put tagline at the end of the quotation):

4. "Education does not pose as insurance against error and sin" (8). (tagline before the quotation):

5. "The world of men must manage itself. With education it can be wiser, but deeper things decide its fate" (8). (tagline at the end of quotation):

6. "Modesty in an educator bases itself, furthermore, upon his perception that accident plays a high role in the affairs of human life, including the affairs of education" (9). (put tagline within the quotation):

CHAPTER 5

Principles of Reader Expectations

The human language, once it is admitted to be complex, reveals itself as cogent. (Mark Van Doren, *Liberal Education* 77)

Goals:

- Understand the expectations of both student and academic readers.

Outcomes:

- Explain the difference between civilian and academic readers.
- Use reader expectations to analyze a text or revise text.

Terms to Know:

- Principles of Reader Expectations (PRE)
- Academic reader
- Civilian reader
- Locations of subjects and verbs
- Identities of subjects and verbs
- Contract
- Old-to-new expectation
- Nominalizations
- Secondary subject–verb combinations

J ust as you found out that automatic verbal activity is going on below the surface of your consciousness, you also have unarticulated expectations about the sentences and paragraphs that you read, as do all readers. These expectations are concerned with the structures of sentences and paragraphs, and I call them the Principles of Reader Expectations (PRE).

In addition, this chapter covers the two kinds of readerships students will encounter while in college: civilian and academic. Students come into college with what I call *civilian expectations,* but in college they must now read the writings of academics who in some ways have expectations—*academic expectations*—about a sentence that are very different from the expectations of the civilian. Most students will not stay in academia after they earn a degree and will instead return to the "civilian" world, yet while in college, they must read academic texts and also write essays that follow academic expectations.

This chapter will help you understand the differences in expectations that civilians and academics have about the structure of sentences. As it turns out, there is only one area where they substantially differ: the identities of subjects and verbs. In all other areas—location of subjects and verbs and paragraph structure, for example—both readerships share the same expectations or preferences.

If you think of a sentence or a paragraph as an IMAX screen, this structure of the sentence (or paragraph) and the functions of the parts are the ribbing behind the screen that keep it up. You don't see the ribbing unless lights behind the screen are turned on, but that ribbing is there, even as the images on the screen change. Similarly, you don't recognize the structure of the sentence or the paragraph until you ask questions about it. These Principles of Reader Expectations have vocabulary that will shine light on the structure of the sentence, regardless of the words embedded in that sentence, and the same thing applies to the paragraph.

Principles of Reader Expectations for the Sentence (Civilian and Academic) (Abbreviated Form)

1. Civilian and academic readers expect (or prefer) the first major grammatical subject–verb combo of a sentence to occur early in the sentence, within the first 7 to 10 words of the sentence (allowing for short introductions).

2. Civilian and academic readers expect (or prefer) this grammatical subject and its verb to be close together in the sentence (few if any words in between them).

3. Civilian readers expect (or prefer) the grammatical subjects of sentences to be actors performing the action of the verbs, whereas academic readers understand that there are reasons to make the grammatical subjects receivers of the actions of the verbs.

4. Civilian readers expect (or prefer) that subjects be flesh-and-blood actor/subjects, whereas academic readers will often prefer non-human subjects (for a variety of valid reasons).

5. In either readership, it is expected that the verb will convey action, whether passive voice or active voice is being used.

Principles of Reader Expectations for the Paragraph (Civilian and Academic) (Abbreviated Form)

1. Both readerships expect a paragraph to begin with a contract, or what is often referred to as the topic sentence. In this framework, the topic sentence is the "contract."

2. Both readerships expect each sentence after the contract to begin with familiar information before that sentence gives new information.

3. Both readerships understand that this familiar information often comes from one of the three elements of the contract, although the familiar information could come from earlier paragraphs or the general topic, or from the new information in the sentence that immediately precedes it.

4. Both readerships expect that new information at the end of the sentence to be significant.

5. Both expect that, as a whole, the beginnings of sentences in a paragraph will refer to a limited but related set of topical subjects.

6. Furthermore, both readerships expect the latter parts of sentences to contain information pertaining to a limited but related set of topics.

Principles of Reader Expectations about Sentences and Paragraphs (Long Form)

1. Civilian and academic readers expect (or prefer) the first major grammatical subject–verb (SV) combo of a sentence to occur early in the sentence, within the first 7 to 10 words of the sentence (allowing for short introductions).

   OBSERVANCE: After class, **the teacher rewrote** this document, even though later she changed her mind about it.

   VIOLATION: <u>Unclear writing puts the first major subject–verb combo late in the sentence:</u> "After class, though later changing her mind about it, seeing how things are different now, the **teacher rewrote** the paper."

2. Civilian and academic readers expect (or prefer) this grammatical subject and its verb to be close together in the sentence (few if any words in between them).

   OBSERVANCE: The **teacher wrote** this document.

   VIOLATION: <u>Many times unclear writing is produced by not following this expectation:</u> **"People** who had bad experiences while growing up and did not listen to the teacher or the teacher wasn't very good at teaching **don't do** well in college."

3. Civilian readers expect (or prefer) the grammatical subjects of sentences to be actors performing the action of the verbs, whereas academic readers understand that there are reasons to make the grammatical subjects receivers of the actions of the verbs.

   Civilian Preference: The teacher wrote this document.

   Academic Preference: The document was written by the teacher.

4. Civilian readers expect (or prefer) that subjects be flesh-and-blood actor/subjects, whereas academic readers will often prefer non-human subjects (for a variety of valid reasons).

   Civilian Preference: Students expect teachers to know their content.

   Academic Preference: Fields of study congregate around core assumptions.

5. In either readership, it is expected that the verb will convey action, whether passive voice or active voice is being used. NOTICE: Action verbs are used in either active or passive voice, although passive voice almost always has a helping verb, some form of "is."

   Civilian Preference: We observed how the solution changed after we inserted the new element.

   Academic Preference: Observations were made after the new element was inserted into the solution.

6. Both readerships expect a paragraph to begin with a contract, what is often referred to as the topic sentence. In this framework, the topic sentence is the "contract."

   a. In this contract we expect to identify a character that will be central to the focus of the paragraph.

   b. We expect to identify a concept that the character is concerned with.

   c. We expect to identify the significance of the character and concept and their relationship to each other.

7. Both readerships expect each sentence after the contract to begin with familiar information before that sentence gives new information.

    a. Each sentence after a contract follows the "old-to-new" principle.

    b. A paragraph that seems choppy or disconnected likely has sentences that go "new to old" or "new to new."

    c. A paragraph that seems to go nowhere as if its "wheels are spinning" likely has sentences that go "old to old."

8. Both readerships understand that this familiar information often comes from one of the three elements of the contract, although the familiar information could come from earlier paragraphs or the general topic, or from the new information in the sentence that immediately precedes it.

    a. NOTE: The familiar information is most often in the subject of the first subject–verb combination

    b. Often, too, EVERY subject of all SV combinations contains familiar information.

9. Both readerships expect that new information at the end of the sentence to be significant.

    VIOLATION: <u>A sentence that has new but weak information at the end has a sense of anti-climax, of ending flat:</u>

    Incorrect Sentence: The process came to a grinding close before we got started.

    Correct Sentence: Before we could even get started, the process came to a grinding halt.

10. Both expect that as a whole, the beginnings of sentences in a paragraph refer to a limited but related set of topical subjects.

    a. So in a 7 sentence paragraph about students and rules, we'd expect the first grammatical subjects of sentences to refer most of the time to students.

11. Furthermore, both Readerships expect the latter parts of sentences to contain information pertaining to a limited but related set of topics.

    a. So, with regards to these 7 sentences, the new information would mostly deal with a couple rules,

NOMINALIZATIONS

What they are:

1. **Nouns that are derived from verbs are called n*ominalizations*.**

   a. Any verb can become a nominalization, that is, a noun.

   b. Being a noun, a nominalization can be used as a grammatical subject.

Examples of nominalizations in the subject position:

1. Here are some examples of nominalizations in the subject position followed by their revisions:

   a. Revisions of this paper were done by me.........I revised this paper.

   b. Inventions of great promise were done by Edison..........Edison invented machines of great promise.

   c. Expectations were high among the fans about their team..........The fans expected their team to win.

To REPEAT:

1. Nouns that are derived from verbs are called nominalizations.

2. Being a noun, a nominalization could be a subject with a verb.

Problems with nominalizations:

1. Because the nominalization is derived from a verb, you have an action (as subject) performing an action, or you have an action receiving an action.

2. This is a level of abstraction that gives abstraction a bad name.

3. When you find you used a nominalization in the subject position, decide if the nominalization is causing unnecessary wordiness in the sentence.

4. There are legitimate uses for nominalizations in the subject position, but for now, I would like you to just be able to identify when a nominalization is in the subject position.

MOST COMMON SOURCES OF BAD WRITING BY CIVLIIAN AND ACADEMIC WRITERS

1. A cause for much unclear or boring academic writing is the **overuse** of nominalizations, especially in subject positions.

2. In addition, the overuse of passive-voice verbs also produces a lot of boring academic and civilian writing.

3. CAUTION: There are legitimate uses for nominalizations and passive-voice verbs, so the key is that you know you are using them and you can justify their use.

4. Nominalizations and passive-voice verbs are cited as the two most common causes of boring and unclear, dense academic writing.

Variables within the Structures of a Sentence

Sentence-structure variables include the following. Note that the * refers to what **civilian** readers expect or prefer.

Subject—could be:
  *Actor
  Receiver
  Described
Verb—could be of TWO kinds:
  1. *Action, and action could be:
      Passive
      *Active
      OR
  2. State of being (e.g., *is, has,* etc.)—could act as
      Equal sign   (e.g., History is bunk.)
      Helping verb   (e.g., I am reading history; war is fought over women.)
Beginning of sentences—could be:
  *Old
  New
Post-beginning of sentences—could be:
  Old
  *New
New stuff at end of sentences—could be:
  *Significant
  Insignificant

Recognize two types of subject–verb combos:

1. The two types are the main (or primary) subject–verb (SV) combination and the secondary SV combination.

2. For shorthand, I will refer to a main SV combination as a **main SV combo**.

3. I will refer to a secondary SV combination as a **secondary SV combo, a secondary**, or a **2ndary**.

4. All SV combos are main combos unless the SV combo is found between another SV combo.

5. The SV combo that splits up another SV combo is a secondary SV combo.

6. Here are three examples of sentences with a 2ndary SV combo (the secondary is in bold, and the main SV is in italics):

   a. *Adults* **who study** hard *learn* very important lessons about life.

   b. *Studying* **what was taught** to us long ago *seems* to be unnecessary.

   c. The *weather* **that** <u>he said</u> **would spoil** our plans *never materialized*. (Actually, here an SV combo splits a secondary SV combo—I call that SV combo a *tertiary SV combo*; notice that you still understand the sentence content.)

7. There is nothing automatically wrong with using secondary SV combos (or tertiary SV combos!), but such animals will cause a main verb to be somewhat farther away from its subject than both civilian and academic readers prefer.

8. In any case, what is totally **unacceptable** is the adult writer not recognizing when he or she is using such SV combos.

The following sentences meet academic readership preferences:

The analysis of the various strands of relativity is the analysis of the social structure of the Universe, as in this epoch. (Whitehead, *Adventures of Ideas* 376)

Our perception of the geometrical order of the Universe brings with it the denial of the restrictions of inheritance to mere personal order. (Ibid 242).

I suggest that the development of systematic theology should be accompanied by a critical understanding of the relation of linguistic expression to our deepest and most persistent intuitions. (Ibid 242).

To a religion which leaves God more or less aloof in the beyond, to be known only by the instructions and commands which come to us from Him, the teaching of the commandment is the primary thing, and the only importance which the bearer of them need have for is that he is the conduit through which the communication has reached us. (Baillie, The *Idea of Revelation* 82)

Despite these very serious drawbacks, I would like to try to retrieve the "cognitive process" of composing as an important site for deepening understanding about the nature of literacy. (Brandt)

Insights into the metacommunicative foundations of literacy help to resolve the paradox with which this study began, revealing social involvement as not merely a cultural impetus for literacy but its interpretive underpinning as well. (Brandt)

THE LESSON: I'm not saying that these sentences should have been revised for civilian PRE; I'm only providing examples of the type of academic writing that the student often faces in the very first week of college—without knowledge of PRE, the student's attention will quickly slip off the rock of comprehension. But, if students are aware of expectations they have about sentences, they have begun to sharpen the claws of verbal engagement such that they can sink their teeth into any text they encounter, tough skinned as the text's PRE might be (mixing of metaphors intended!).

CHAPTER 6

Flush-Left Diagramming: A Tool for Rereading and Revising

The powers of the person are what education wishes to perfect. To aim at anything less is to belittle men. His mind has its own laws, which are the laws of thought. *(Mark Van Doren, Liberal Education 40).*

Goals:

- Understand flush-left diagramming (FLD) as a tool for identifying sources of wordiness in sentences.
- Understand how FLD can help the reader to understand difficult texts.
- Begin to memorize the variables in sentence structure that readers will tolerate.

Outcomes:

- Know the definitions of grammatical terms that refer to the relationships of the parts of a sentence.
- Demonstrate understanding of the rules of FLD.
- Explain the three kinds of structure in a sentence.
- Practice converting a sentence to FLD form and identifying sentence features in the light of reader expectations about sentence structure.

Terms to Know:

- Infinitives
- Relative Pronouns
- Helping Verbs
- silent' relative pronoun-helping verb
- Nominalizations
- Main Subject-verb combinations
- Secondary Subject-verb combinations
- Brackets

Note: These pages convey lots of detail, so refer to them often while doing flush-left diagramming (FLD).

I propose that students can improve their chances of attaining an adult-level engagement with words by using the activity I created called flush-left diagraming (FLD). It serves as a dissection instrument, making it easier to see the "regulatory" systems of the sentence. Because the sentence is the smallest verbal unit that conveys meaning, writers who can develop flexibility in constructing sentences so that diverse audiences are reached with the same content will feel an intellectual strength that is the birthright of any human adult.

Comments

I came up with this activity after seeing that the first reader expectations deal with the **locations** of subjects and verbs. To review, remember that readers—both civilian and academic—like verbs near their subjects and the first subject–verb (SV) combination near the start of a sentence.

On the basis of this expectation about the locations of subjects and verbs, the following occurred to me:

1. You can break up any sentence so that it looks like a traditional poem, with every other line indented.

2. But the lines that begin flush left are in that position due to certain rules:
   a. The first word must be the subject (and so a noun), and
   b. the last word on that line must be its verb.

3. Then, all the words after that verb (if there are more words) go on the indented line right below that prior line.

4. On that indented line, you write all the words that occur before the next main SV combination—if there is another main SV combination.

5. If there is another SV combination, you begin a flush-left line right below that indented line.

6. Again, the first word of the flush-left line has to be a noun, because a subject is a noun, and then that subject's verb ends that line.

7. You keep going in this manner until you get to the end of the sentence.

Now, FLD does require that you be able to identify subjects and verbs, but keep this in mind: I provide you with a process for identifying subjects and verbs such that you can check your work to make sure you identified real subjects and verbs. So just like in the first stage of writing, you won't be bummed out if you were mistaken in your first attempts to identify subjects and verbs. Also, this means that you can expect to "raise your batting average," so that by the end of the course you will have gone from correctly identifying subjects and verbs 20 percent of the time to being right (in the end) 80 to 90 to 100 percent of the time. (And don't you think society would expect that of college-educated students?)

Flush-Left Rules: To Repeat Them

A key feature of sentences is how they have a structure that is separate from the words that are embedded in that structure. I try to illustrate this concept visually with the second wedge on the inside front cover of the textbook. FLD can help you to literally see this structure, although you have to know where the subjects and verbs are before you can use FLD with a sentence. Later, you will see that when you use FLD with sentences that are not clear to you, you will understand the content of the passage and you can see how that writer is violating reader expectations! So, this activity can help you with both rewriting and rereading.

Instructions for Diagramming Sentences Using the Flush-Left Concept

1. Take any sentence and break it up like a poem, with every other line indented—but, each line that is flush left begins with a main subject and ends with the main subject's verb.

2. Then, **on the indented line,** put all the words that follow the main verb and occur before the next main subject.

3. Next, put that new subject as the first word of the next flush-left line and end that line with its verb.

4. Because there are fewer verbs than nouns (and a subject is always a noun), **first** look for verbs and then find the subject (which is ordinarily **in front of a verb** in prose).

5. Be aware of **secondary verbs**, which are positioned between a main subject and verb, so that they divide what readers like to have together. (This is another reason to look for verbs first.)

6. If there is a secondary subject and verb in the sentence, you will find two verbs without a subject between them, and then the first subject you find will be the secondary subject.

7. But remember, each line that begins flush left starts with a **main** subject and ends with that subject's verb.

8. Also, don't start the flush-left line with articles like *a* or *the*, and don't start them with adjectives—only start them with the main subject-noun.

Variables to Be Aware of in Flush-Left Diagramming

It is important to know that the Principles of Reader Expectations (PRE) are expectations or preferences and not iron-clad rules. The reader (you, me, and others) can understand when these expectations are violated, but as writers, you will be able to produce more powerful final drafts when you know when you are violating PRE and can explain your reasons for doing so. To explain variable structures within sentences, you must use the vocabulary of the grammatical terms and of PRE. That is why you should **memorize** these terms and variables as quickly as possible. The Default Questions section later in the chapter also deals with these variables.

Recognize Two Types of Subject–Verb Combos:

a. The two types are main (or primary) and secondary.

b. For shorthand, I will refer to a main SV combo as an SV combo, and I will refer to a secondary SV combo as a **secondary SV combo, a secondary, or a 2ndary.**

c. A secondary SV combo is called secondary because it is located between a main subject and its verb.

d. This means that a flush-left line can have more than one SV combo, but it will have **only one** main SV combo; there can be one or more secondary SV combos.

Identify Infinitives:

a. These are verbs that have the word *to* in front of them. Don't confuse them with actual verbs (what I call *Verb-verbs*).

b. You should experiment with changing infinitives into verbs when revising to see if your sentence is stronger with the infinitives as verbs.

c. In addition, you can improve your vocabulary by changing infinitives into verbs.

Identify Relative Pronouns:

a. Relative pronouns are words like *who*, *that*, and *which*.

b. They come right after a noun that you might think is the subject, but the relative pronoun—standing in for that noun—is the subject.

c. CAUTION: The relative pronoun can be a main subject or a secondary subject.

Recognize Helping Verbs:

a. Before you make a flush-left line end with *is* or *were*, check the next words that follow the is verb to see if an action verb appears (within a few words).

b. If so, that *is* verb is a helping verb and should not end the flush-left line.

Recognize "Silent" Relative Pronoun–Helping Verb Situations:

a. Sometimes a noun next to what appears to be a verb is not really an SV combination but is a kind of shorthand SV combo that shouldn't be moved flush left.

b. Such formations leave out the relative pronoun and the helping verb.

c. They don't occur often, but enough that you need to be sensitive to this format.

d. You might sometimes decide to include the "silent partners" in your final draft.

e. Example: "The student wrote essays filled with gems of metaphors."

    1. There is a silent relative pronoun and helping verb between *essays* and *filled*.

    2. With these inserted into the sentence, the sentence would be: "The student wrote essays *that were* filled with gems of metaphors."

Recognize Nominalizations:

a. Nominalizations are nouns that are derived from verbs.

b. Because it is a noun, a nominalization could be a subject with a verb.

c. Because the nominalization is derived from a verb, there is an *action* in the place of an actor/subject performing an action, or an action receiving an action.

d. This is a level of abstraction that gives abstraction a bad name.

e. There are legitimate uses for nominalizations in the subject position, but for now, I would like you to just be able to identify when a nominalization is in the subject position.

f. But be aware that a cause of much unclear or boring academic writing is the OVERUSE of nominalizations, especially in subject positions.

g. That and the overuse of passive-voice verbs are cited as the two most common causes of boring academic writing.

In the following section, you will find explanations of other aspects of words that will come up as you attempt to use FLD with sentences. Much of this information might not sink into your head right now, but keep this section in mind as you go through the rest of the book.

Default Questions

Following are questions that you should ask yourself to determine the identity of various parts of a sentence before you can use FLD. This list is incomplete, but it should help you in your rookie season of FLD.

To determine if a *be* verb is the main verb or helping verb, ASK: Is there an action verb right after this verb or within a word or two?

- If not, this *be* verb is the main verb and ends a flush-left line.
- If there is an action verb after it, then the *be* verb is a helping verb and the flush-left line ends with the main verb.

Example:

He is writing more than he is talking, which was his goal.

1. NOTE: Here the word after *is* is an action word, and it is a verb-verb (writing; talking).

   a. A test for this is to use a form of *writing* and *talking* without *is*—then you'd come up with "he writes more than he talks."

2. There is a third verb in this example, the past-tense form of *is*—*was*. But there is no verb after *was*, only a possessive pronoun followed by a noun—*goal*—so this verb is the main verb, and *is* is a helping verb.

Using FLD, the sentence would be as follows:

He is writing
    more than
he is talking,
which was
    his goal.

ANOTHER EXAMPLE:

It is often that we stumble before we fly.

Here, there are three SV combinations, and the first main verb is *is* and its subject is *It*—obvious enough. Constructions such as *it is*, or *there are* contain "empty subjects," and they are used for rhetorical purposes, to emphasize what is to come. Here is the sentence using FLD:

It is
    often that
we stumble
    before
we fly.

ANOTHER EXAMPLE:

There are times when we despair of ever flying.

This is another example of an empty SV combination, and again it has the rhetorical purpose of announcing that an important idea is about to be presented. Here is the sentence using FLD:

There are
    times when
we despair
    of ever flying.

To determine if *that* is being used as a conjunction or a relative pronoun, ASK: Does *that* follow a verb or a noun?

- If it follows a verb, then *that* is a conjunction and will likely begin an indented line.
- If it follows a noun, it likely is a relative pronoun that is referring to the noun right in front of it. In this case:
  - *That* is the main subject and begins a flush-left line.
  - The noun that it refers to is placed on the indented line (probably the last word of the indented line).

Example of *that* being a conjunction:

I think that I will eventually understand flush-left diagraming.

We read so many books that we looked like worms.

Example of *that* being a relative pronoun and subject:

Flush-left diagramming is an activity that makes my head hurt.

Example of sentence that uses *that* both ways:

We read so many books that we looked like worms, and those were worms that attracted fish and birds.

Here are the four previous example sentences using FLD:

I think
    that
I will eventually understand
    flush left diagraming.

We read
    so many books that
we looked
    like worms.

    Flush left
diagramming is
    an activity
that makes
    my head hurt.

We read
    so many books that
we looked
    like worms and
those were
    worms
that attracted
    fish and birds.

Important to Note:

1. There are two other relative pronouns (besides *that*) that adult writers should be aware of: *who* and *which*.

2. All three relative pronouns stand in for a noun, and these pronouns are usually the grammatical subjects of SV combinations.

3. So whenever you find one of these relative pronouns in front of a verb, it is likely the grammatical subject, and the noun it refers to will likely be the word just in front of the pronoun.

4. This noun, though, will be the last word of the indented line just above the next flush-left line.

5. Refer to the two previous flush-left sentences: In the last sentence, *that* refers to *worms* and *worms* is the indented word; in the penultimate sentence, *that* refers to *activity*, which is on the line above it.

To determine if a noun is a subject, ASK: Is it part of a prepositional phrase?

- That is, does a preposition come before it, within two or three words?
- If so, that noun cannot be a subject.
- Take out all of the words between it and what seems to be its verb.

Examples:

The solutions to enduring problems that are forcing men of goodwill to get panicky exist within those panicky adults.

Explanation: The first verb is *are forcing* and its subject is *that*, but when you look for another verb you find *exist*. Its subject must be in front of the verb, and yet the nouns are *will*, *men*, *problems*, and *solutions*. With each noun, except the last one listed, either the noun is part of a prepositional phrase or it is the object of a verb (*men*). This means *solutions* is the subject for *exist*.

Following is this sentence using FLD. Two things to notice: (1) the main verb is pretty far from its subject, and (2) there is a secondary SV splitting the main SV.

The
solutions to enduring problems that are forcing men of good will to get panicky exist
    within those panicky adults.

Not sure if a word is a verb? Do this:

- Use it in its own sentence as a verb, and create a subject for it.
- See if it makes grammatical sense, or "sounds right."

For example, I'm wondering if the word *familiar* is a verb in this sentence:
We can get familiar with these rules.
To find out, I intentionally use it as a verb in a different sentence:
I familiar with these rules.
Notice that this does not sound correct and the word cannot be easily—or maybe ever!—used as a verb. So this sentence's flush-left form would be:

We can get
    familiar with these rules.

Checking Your Work

When you produce a flush-left diagram, you can check your work like you used to do when learning subtraction and addition. Here are some ways to check your work to determine whether your flush-left diagram is correct:

1. A flush left-line **always**, always has at least two words in it (the subject and its verb). So you ask yourself:

2. Is the first flush-left word a noun?

3. If so, it is likely the subject—but, check the following:

   a. Make sure you didn't put an adjective as the first flush-left word, thinking that because it modifies the subject, it should start the flush-left line.

   b. Make sure you didn't make the subject a noun that is the object of a preposition or a transitive verb.

4. Then you ask: Is the last flush-left word the **main** verb?

   a. If so, you likely have the right verb. But be careful with *is* verbs (and forms of is, such as *was*, *were*, etc.).

   b. To know if it should be at end of the flush-left line, you have to determine if it *is* a helping verb or a main verb.

5. Are there any verb-verbs on an indented line?

   a. If you a verb-verb on an indented line, then you need to restructure the diagram.

   b. There can never be a verb-verb on a properly diagramed flush-left sentence.

6. Any flush-left line can have more than one SV combo on it, because secondary SV combos can split up a main SV combo.

   a. So there can be several SV combos on a flush-left line.

   b. But there is only one main SV combo.

7. Because each SV combination is grammatically correct, each could have a period after it.

   a. So, treat each combo as a sentence—if it sounds grammatically correct, it probably is.

   b. For example, "He spoke" is a simple sentence and would be correctly placed by itself on a flush-left line.

   c. "Him spoke" is grammatically incorrect and would not be on a flush-left line.

Here is an **abbreviated version** of the list of questions to ask to determine if your flush left diagram is correct:

1. Is the verb preceded by to? *If so, it can't be a verb-verb; it's an infinitive.*

2. Is a noun preceded by a preposition? *If so, it can't be the subject, although it is a noun. Look for a noun before the preposition—it likely is the subject.*

3. Is the first word in your flush-left line a noun?

4. Is the last word of your flush-left line a verb?

5. Does the phrase that is flush left make grammatical sense?

6. Is a silent *to* or a silent relative pronoun + helping verb in play?

A Comment About the Utility of Flush-Left Diagramming

Most students, and people in general, don't reflect much on how they write, or know how to determine and describe the quality of their writing beyond vague and (often) inaccurate pronouncements. I think that students can describe the quality of their writing more accurately when they use the vocabulary of PRE, and the vocabulary of PRE can help students create the FLD.

When you can identify subjects and verbs in sentences and use FLD, you can see graphically the location of subjects and verbs in relation to each other, and you can understand better why sentences are considered clear or unclear. When sentences are unclear, you can see the nature of their weaknesses and unpack their meaning. Thus, I hope that you take the time to master this analytical and descriptive tool.

In addition, when you are revising sentences in your own writing, FLD can be very helpful if you sense that a sentence is wordy or vague but you can't spot the problems in a straight-line sentence format. When you break up a sentence to look like a poem, you can see the parts of the sentence more easily. The flush-left diagram is like a dissection of a frog—you can see the "internal" systems of the sentence, the grammatical and rhetorical systems, as well as things like infinitives, normalizations, and words that convey action but aren't verb-verbs.

Even more interesting, you can use this tool to unpack sentences you read in textbooks that aren't easy to understand. Remember that any declarative sentence is likely grammatically correct, so there are subjects and verbs in the dense forest of that academic sentence. You can hunt them down and pin them into a flush-left diagram. Even if you don't understand the specialized wording, the process of FLD might help you understand the content of the sentence.

The PRE terms and FLD help you see all the options you have within yourself to revise your writing to (1) make the writing more concrete and accurate, (2) meet the reading preferences of your audience, (3) perhaps wow any audience with your word choices and sentence structures that walk a thin line between violating their preferences and meeting the expectations of a larger audience—that of the human intellect.

Types of Flush-Left Diagrams You Will Need to Produce

Following you will find many sentences in flush-left form. Study how the diagrams meet the rules for FLD and PRE:

1. Notice that the first words that begin flush-left lines are nouns.

2. Notice that these nouns are grammatical subjects.

3. Notice that the last word on each flush-left line is the verb for that subject.

4. Notice how close each verb is to its subject—both civilian and academic readers like subjects near their verbs.

5. Notice that there is **never** a Verb-verb on an indented line if the sentence has been flushed left correctly.

You want to have a method for revising, so that you will spend your time smartly.

You want
    to have a method for revising, so
you will spend
    your time smartly.

Comments: The verbs are near their subjects; there is an infinitive—*to have*—which isn't a Verb-verb, so it is indented.

> *The key is to not spend too much time on any part of the early stages.*

    The

key is

    to not spend too much time on any part of the early stages.

Comments: The main verb is *is,* so we call it an **equal sign verb;** an infinitive follows the main verb.

> *Even in factual papers, a lot of creativity goes into it—although I prefer the word "imagination" to "creativity."*

    Even in factual papers, a

lot of creativity goes

    into it—although

I prefer

    the word "imagination" to "creativity."

Comments: The first subject is a common noun—lot—and to test it, you drop the words between it and what seem to be its verbs. You then have "a lot ... goes into...." This is grammatically correct.

> Having an "imaginative literacy" involves seeing this.

    Having an "imaginative literacy" involves

      seeing this.

Comments: Here a nominalization is the subject, but it could be a verb. It can be acceptable to have nominalizations such as this in the subject position, although two things must be kept in mind: (1) too many of these forms consecutively in a passage could produce vague writing, and (2) you should always know that you are using such kinds of nouns in the subject position and have good reason for doing so.

How A Flush-Left Diagram Looks When You Have Many Words Between The Verb and The Next Subject

> *Perhaps nothing shows more clearly the enormous forces of production constantly going to waste than the fact that the most prosperous time in all branches of business that this country has known was during the Civil War, when we were maintaining great fleets and armies, and millions of our industrial population were engaged in supplying them with wealth for unproductive consumption or for reckless destruction.*

                Perhaps

nothing shows

                more clearly the enormous forces of production constantly going to waste than
                the fact that the most prosperous

time in all branches of business that this country has known was

                during the Civil War, when

we were maintaining

                great fleets and armies, and

millions of our industrial population were engaged

                in supplying them with wealth for unproductive consumption or for reckless
                destruction.

Note: When not all the words for **an indented line** can be on one line, begin the second line where you started the first indented line.

How a Flush-Left Diagram Looks When The Sentence Has Secondary Subject–Verb Combinations

*The date of the flood layer that **Woolley discovered** was considered too old to co-incide with the biblical account of the flood, but matched up much better with the older Mesopotamian tale.*

                The

date of the flood layer that **Woolley discovered** was considered

                too old to coincide with the biblical account of the flood, but

[it] matched

                up much better with the older Mesopotamian tale.

Comments: the SV combo "Woolley discovered" splits up the main SV—"Date... was considered." Also note that because at least two words have to be on a flush-left line, I put in brackets a noun that refers to the subject—[it]. The brackets indicate that the word is not in the original sentence, and its use shows the writer that the final draft might include that subject.

A key breakthrough **we should reflect** on is that sentences have a structure that is separate from the words that are embedded in that structure.

                A key

breakthrough **we should reflect** on is

                that

sentences have

                a structure

that is

     separate from the words

that are embedded

     in that structure.

How a Flush Left Diagram Looks When a Main Verb is far from its Subject

> *Tropology is especially useful for the analysis of narrative historiography because narrative history is a mode of discourse in which the relations between what a given culture regards as literal truths and the figurative truths expressed in its characteristic fiction, the kinds of stories it tells about itself and others, can be tested.*
> (Hayden White, Figural Realism 18)

Tropology is

     especially useful for the analysis of narrative historiography because narrative

history is

     a mode of discourse in which the

relations between what a given culture regards as literal truths and the figurative

                    truths expressed

                       in its

                    characteristic

                      fiction,

                      the

                      kinds

                      of

                      stories

                      it tells

                      about

                      itself

                      and

                      others,

                      can be

                      tested.

Note: To emphasize how far the verb is from its subject, I stack words below the last word that is flush to the right and then the last word of that column is the verb—in this case *tested*, and its subject is *relations*. Imagine there is a tightrope between the subject and verb that helps the reader get through the content of the sentence. If the verb is far from its subject, it is like that tightrope is really long and saggy, and the reader thus finds it difficult to remain focused on the content of the sentence and might fall off the bandwagon or lose interest. Here's one more example:

> In historical narratives, the dominant plot forms utilized by a culture to imagine the different kinds of meaning (tragic, comic, epic, farcical, etc.) which a distinctively human form of life **might have** are tested against the information and knowledge that specific forms of human life **have had** in the past.

In historical narratives, the dominant plot
forms utilized by a culture to imagine the different kinds of meaning (tragic, comic, epic,
farcical, etc.)
which a
distinctively
human
form
of life
might
have
are
tested

against the information and knowledge that specific
forms of human life **have had**
in the past.

Examples of when you need to insert brackets for flush-left diagraming

You must strictly follow the rule that all flush-left lines must first have a subject and then a verb. But when you have a compound verb (one subject is stated but two verbs are stated), then you need to repeat that subject in the flush-left form, even though it doesn't appear in the original sentence. To show this, after you flush left the subject and verb that are stated in the sentence, put the *and* that is between the two verbs on the indented line and then start another flush-left line. Place the repeated subject (or a proper replacement) **in brackets** on this flush-left line, then write in the second verb. Brackets are only used with repeated subjects and are only found at the start of flush-left lines. Here are some examples:

Example 1:

> *The students wrote and typed up the response.*

> The
> students wrote
> and
> [they] typed
> up the response.

Note: You could also repeat "the students," but then be careful:

> The
> students wrote
> and [the
> [students] typed
> up the response.

Example 2:

Note: Sometimes the subject consists of several words, and then you can use a pronoun in brackets:

> *The date of the flood layer that **Woolley discovered** was considered too old to coincide with the biblical account of the flood, but matched up much better with the older Mesopotamian tale.*

> The
> date of the flood layer that **Woolley discovered** was considered
> too old to coincide with the biblical account of the flood, but
> [it] matched
> up much better with the older Mesopotamian tale.

Example 3:

> Before too long, we had written more than we had expected and so forgot to call the teacher.

> Before too long,
> we had written
> more than
> we had expected
> and so
> [we] forgot
> to call the teacher.

Note: When you identify the need to repeat a subject in brackets, you shouldn't assume that the sentence was originally weak without that stated subject. However, now you can decide if the sentence works better that way.

FLD Practice: Indented Line Pushing

NAME: .... CLASS HOUR: .... DATE: ....

In the following sentences, all lines are set flush left; rewrite so that the correct lines are indented.

Example:

It's
not that
we don't want
a first draft to be perfect, but the
nature of things is
such that
this rarely happens.

Correct Form:

It's
        not that
we don't want
        a first draft to be perfect, but the
nature of things is
        such that
this rarely happens.

1.

But with enough practice of this procedure,
you do find
that your first
drafts are
qualitatively better than first drafts that
you'd done
in the past.

1.

2.

The
key is
to not dawdle on any part of the early stages.

2.

3.

You also want
to have a method for revising, so your
time is spent
smartly.

3.

4.   **4.**

After all,
you look
at most reports of "Facts,"
you'll see
that
metaphors are used—

5.   **5.**

Even in factual papers, a
lot of creativity goes
into it—although
I prefer
the word "imagination" to "creativity."

6.   **6.**

The other
thing is
that
it IS
good to have the mechanics correct, but too many
students have
a paper
that has
no "life" to it, though technically
it is
correct.

7.   **7.**

We don't want
boring and technically correct:
we want
lively and technically correct.

8.   **8.**

we can't help
but use metaphors to convey facts, but
we often don't see this.

Although each of the following flush-left diagrams has a main subject (noun) begin-ning each line, each line doesn't end with that subject's verb. Find the verb and indent the remaining words on each line as needed.

Example:

You will begin to see that our
intellect uses a metaphor to produce a coherent understanding of something, but
that doesn't mean that
we have the wisest and most realistic understanding of something.

Correct flush-left diagram:

> You will begin
>> to see that our
> intellect uses
>> a metaphor to produce a coherent understanding of something, but
> that doesn't mean
>> that
> we have
>> the wisest and most realistic understanding of something.

1.

We achieve this highest level after

we have exploited the metaphorical resources of a word, and

[we have] come to understand how a realistic

explanation of things is presented through the metaphorical dimension of words.

2.

I hope

we will have experienced the perfect writing process too, the one that tells us that

we should forgive our early miscues and mistakes, since

that kind of forgiveness releases the powers of our imagination, and the powers of the metaphor.

2.

3.

This means that

we can see our experiences of trial and error as the arena where

we have moments of breakthrough.

4.

We will then develop an imaginative literacy

that will always refresh us and

we will feel a sense of liberation that

we experience as

we cleanse our understanding of errors that

we brought into college.

4.

5.

We then not only have a wise understanding of a topic, but

we have a wise and realistic understanding of the process of understanding.

5.

NAME: .... CLASS HOUR: .... DATE: ....

The following sentences have main verbs located far from their subjects; create a flush-left diagram for each sentence. (Be sure to identify verbs before you look for subjects.) HINT: there are some secondary SV combos in these sentences.

1. Verbally training someone on room set up and handing down verbally and through notes (written or typed in email) the way that teachers have done and are to do duties at ECNS has worked in the past but it is clear that it is no longer the best way based on misunderstandings and poor communication.

1.

2. We will need to understand that this external acceleration of the pace of change – as evident in many ways, but just for exposition purposes, we will refer to the quick outmodedness of computer levels – will beckon or require that the people in commercial civilization be able to develop a mode of intellectual machinations that also has an ability to accelerate the pace of change, intellectually speaking.

3. (from Emerson's "Nature")

Debt, which consumes so much time, which so cripples and disheartens a great spirit with cares that seem so base, is a preceptor whose lessons cannot be forgone, and is needed most by those who suffer from it most

4. Applying the PRE to my other reading assignments by noticing the subject and verb being in theright spot in a sentence has helped me in my writing.

5. Running every day for a couple miles by using the dog for a running mate and barking at him like I'm a dog, too, has proven to be not so helpful.

6. The news her friends were so quick to give her because they feared that how upset she would be and the effect it would have on her heart ended up delivering the bad consequences but not in the way they predicted.

NAME: .... CLASS HOUR: .... DATE: ....

Each of the following sentences has a secondary subject–verb combination; create a flush-left diagram for each sentence.

1. What I wanted to say was that I like reading and writing.

2. Those who like to play with fire tend to burn themselves out quickly.

3. We who read with a CLEW will see images popping out of the words we read on the page.

4. An integral part that ensures the integrity of this Truth is the ability to keep it as a written record.

5. In my opinion, what Koch is trying to make us understand is that we should open our mind and think outside the box when we think of something.

6. One of the first points that Frye explains on what is it like to be a thinker, is his comparison to math.

7. Another thing Frye talks about is unintelligibility.

TEST: Flush-Left Diagramming

NAME: .... CLASS HOUR: .... DATE: ....

Use FLD on the following sentences from a student paper.

1. Society today is also teaching us that the knowledge of literacy can let the average person sneak by in life.

2. Knowing how to read and write is extremely important in society, but somewhere in there we lost the importance of words.

3. I believe Frye is one of the few people that is a deep thinker and his essay is trying to spread his word and attempt to get people to think deeper about their words and the context of all words.

4. Because of this, teachers feel pressured to get their students to understand, but struggle to get them to grasp concepts society doesn't even understand.

5. Society today is also teaching us that the knowledge of literacy can let the average person sneak by in life.

6. I've been involved with Liberal Education at some level since I entered college in the Fall of 1970.

7. And if it is true that humanity is Biology's 2nd matrix of consciousness, then we can try to list the attributes of a 3rd matrix of biological consciousness.

8. You will need a bibliography for each of the articles (chapters) that you used from that anthology.

9. You see that Life asks students to consciously be open to the movements of the spirit as they submit to the rigors of education at the liberation level.

10. The wise man shows his wisdom in separation, in gradation, and his scale of creatures and of merits is as wide as nature. The foolish have no range in their scale, but suppose every man is as every other man.

Activity: Flush-Left Diagramming

NAME: .... CLASS HOUR: .... DATE: ....

Use FLD on the following sentences. Notice that the "skeleton" of the diagram for each sentence is given, so you have to figure out which words go on which lines. For example, if the first line is indented, then you know the first words will be indented. If the first line is flush left, then the first words will be flush left. The "skeleton" gives you a rough idea of how many words are on each line. So, I call this the "Skeletor" activity.

1. Then at the start of the flush left chapter, I refer to the scene of Neo seeing the matrix after going through the death experience.

      _____

  _____

    _____

2. College is the red pill—you aren't in Kansas anymore, the understanding that you got in childhood and which you bring into college.

  _____

    _____

_____

  _____,_____

_____

  _____

_____

  _____.

3. College will cause anxiety, you will have some harrowing experiences, mental battles, but this is just part of the growing up period in adulthood.

  _____

    _____

_____

  _____

_____

_____

4. Then you could scrub errors off the body of understanding that you bring into adulthood from childhood and you see that the scales of inadequate adult thinking fall off your eyes, your consciousness's eyes.

   _____

   _____

   _____

   _____

   _____

   _____

   _____

   _____

   _____

5. As you develop these intellectual-verbal virtues, the vices of lack of confidence and anxiety just shrivel up from non-use.

   _____

   _____

   _____,_____

   _____

   _____

6. You find that the adult does less of the old stuff of being defensive in the face of doubt and threats and more offensive, or active.

   _____

   _____

   _____

   _____

7. And as Morpheus says, you can't be shown the matrix, you have to see it for yourself, you have to test out the claims that college professors say are truthful.

   _____

   _____

   _____

   _____,

   _____

   _____,

   _____

   _____

CHAPTER 7

The Phenomena of Sentences

The conventionalizing of speech known as prose . . . is actually a very difficult and sophisticated convention. (Northrop Frye, *The Critical Path* 144)

Actual prose is the expression or imitation of directed thinking or controlled description in words, and its unit is the sentence. It is not ordinary speech but speech on its best behavior, in its Sunday clothes, aware of an audience and with its relations to that audience prepared beforehand. (Northrop Frye, *The Well-Tempered Critic* 18).

Goals:

- Continue using PRE for sentences, with understanding of the two readerships college students must negotiate: civilian and academic.
- Learn a process for analysis of sentence structure.
- Learn a better way to understand how a sentence conveys meaning.
- Use basic grammatical terms to identify the function of grammatical elements within sentences.
- Know the location and identity preferences of the two readerships.

Outcomes:

- Possess the ability to analyze the structure of a sentence to perceive its observance or violation of expectations preferred by a readership.
- Possess the ability to write a sentence for either readership.

- Explain how and why a sentence gets traction in the reader's mind or why it lacks that trait.
- Revise text to ensure it meets reader preferences at the sentence level.
- Explain how it is that the college student doesn't need a bigger vocabulary in order to write at the academic level.

Terms to Know:

- Adult-level understanding
- Civilian readership
- Academic readership
- Infinitives
- Nominalizations
- Prepositional phrases
- Flush-left diagramming
- Subordinate conjunctions

The Sentence

A college-level education involves becoming aware of the verbal intellectual activity that takes place automatically in the mind, and so in this chapter, you will learn of the unconscious expectations you have about the structure of a sentence. It is important to have this "X-ray" vision about sentence structure because the sentence is the basic verbal unit by which we convey meaning or knowledge. It is also important to realize that this structure we see isn't the grammatical structure. The following sentence wedge (also on the inside front cover of the textbook) might help here:

This sentence wedge can open your eyes to see a structure to sentences that exists apart from the words that are embedded in that structure. Notice that grammatical correctness is only one of three elements in the structure of the sentence. But as everyone knows, a sentence that is grammatically correct might still not be easy to read. The third thread—rhetorical effectiveness—refers to word choice. This factor leads

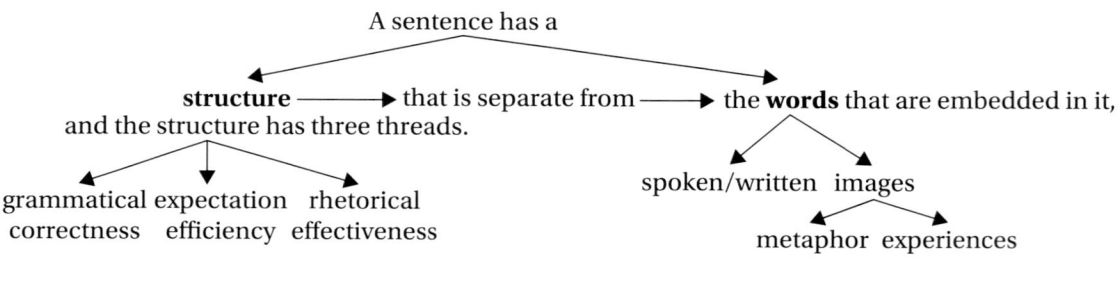

to several variables as well. The middle thread—expectation efficiency—is what this chapter is concerned with. So, the sentences you will analyze in this chapter are grammatically correct and rhetorically effective, but they have fatal flaws associated with efficiency and the expectations readers of sentences bring to the reading of the text. Through the chapter activities, you will learn how to identify and correct these flaws.

Principles of Reader Expectations (PRE)

Here are the expectations that civilian and academic readers have about sentence structure. Notice in what ways they share the same expectations and in what ways they differ.

1. Civilian and academic readers expect (or prefer) the first major grammatical subject–verb (SV) combo of a sentence to occur early in the sentence, within the first 7 to 10 words of the sentence (allowing for short introductions).

2. Civilian and academic readers expect (or prefer) a grammatical subject and its verb to be close together in the sentence (few if any words in between them).

3. Civilian readers expect (or prefer) the grammatical subjects of sentences to be actors performing the action of the verbs, *whereas academic readers understand that there are reasons to make the grammatical subjects receivers of the actions of the verbs.*

4. Civilian readers expect or prefer that subjects be flesh-and-blood actor/subjects, *whereas academic readers often prefer non-human subjects (for a variety of valid reasons).*

5. In either readership, it is expected that the verb will convey action, whether the passive voice or active voice is being used.

In summary, we can say that both readerships have the same preferences with regard to the **location** of subjects and verbs (PRE 1 and 2), but they can differ with regard to the **identities** of subjects and verbs.

It is also important to remember that these preferences are not absolute or mutually exclusive—they simply describe general preferences within specific adult intellectual environments. Being aware of these expectations (or preferences) will improve your chances of knowing that your writing will get traction in the reader's mind, whichever readership it is, and you will know this with a degree of certainty you formerly did not possess.

In addition, use of PRE can help you unpack difficult writing that you must read in your college courses. PRE can help you paraphrase that difficult text, leading to greater understanding of the text's meaning.

The Expectation of Efficiency

These reader expectations deal with the "efficiency" of the sentence, although I'm not entirely happy with that word. Still, it is important to remember that a grammatically correct sentence can still be wordy and vague and generally hard to understand.

Now, in this chapter we will see how these expectations **can help you not only in revising your own writing but in rereading and understanding the difficult writing you encounter in college.**

There are several assumptions underlying the activities in this chapter, and these assumptions have been presented in other chapters. Here I'll just reiterate:

a. Expect your initial observations about sentence structure to change as you study the sentences.

b. Forgive yourself if your early observations are mistaken. You have to start somewhere!

c. Expect your understanding of the topic to likely improve as you revise sentences on the basis of your identification of sentences you guess the reader would have wanted you to revise.

Reading Difficult Academic Prose

Because students in college do more reading of college-level texts before they do any formal writing, let's first examine some sentences by academics that students might find difficult.

Now, suppose you have to understand the following sentence from an academic text because any misunderstanding on your part could trigger a nuclear exchange between superpowers. Here is the sentence:

> *Evidently observation of the earlier stages of personal life will afford the clearest evidence of Peace.* (from *Adventures of Ideas* by A. N. Whitehead, p. 369)

The problem is that you, as a "civilian" reader, are—along with all other civilians—tired of what is perceived to be egghead writing by uppity "brainiacs," and Whitehead's sentence, although its content is important, has a structure that you and other civilians will no longer stomach or tolerate. What will you do?

I'd suggest, first, just to help you see its features, that you should use flush-left diagramming (FLD) with the sentence. Using FLD is like dissecting a sentence that, for the civilian, is already dead on arrival (DOA) before they even set their eyes on the sentence. Here is the sentence using FLD:

> Evidently
> observation of the earlier stages of personal life will afford
>   the clearest evidence of Peace.

Analysis: The most obvious feature is that the single subject is a nominalization, and we will want to change it into a Verb-verb during our revision session.

To do this, ask yourself, *Who observes?* Several answers work here—*we, they, you,* and others.

Another thing to note: What one word could we substitute for "earlier stages of personal life"? [Spoiler alert—I'll mention it right after the bracket here →]: *childhood.*

One other factor to note: We will use a subordinate conjunction to preserve the order of activity and suggest the cause-and-effect relationship that Whitehead is trying to describe.

REVISED SENTENCE:

> *When we observe our childhood, we can see [or observe] the clearest evidence of Peace.*

Note: It is likely that this revision fixes the weaknesses that frustrated the fed-up civilian in the original sentence. If we use FLD with the revised sentence, we see more graphically how close the verbs are to the subject, and FLD shows that the sentence follows civilian preferences for identities of subjects and verbs:

> When
> we observe
>   our childhood,
> we can see
>   the clearest evidence of Peace.

Note: This is just one way to revise a sentence when you know your audience finds nominalizations in subject positions to be repugnant to their sense of style and grace. The educated adult should be able to produce sentence structures that meet what the audience prefers.

Here is another sentence that the civilian might feel he or she must "decode" in order to prevent "the end" from arriving (or, to bring about the end of inadequate adult writing **in a final draft**):

> *The question here for discussion is how the intuition of Peace asserts itself apart from its disclosure in tragedy.*

Comment: This is another sentence from Whitehead (p. 369), and before we revise it, let's dissect it using FLD so that we can see the three threads that make up the sentence's structure:

> The
> question here for discussion is
>   how the
> intuition of Peace asserts
>   itself apart from its disclosure in tragedy.

Analysis: Again, this is a beautiful sentence, if you like nominalizations in subject positions and no mention of humans, even though they are doing the actions implied in the words. (In other words, if you are Joe or Jane Academic.)

The remarkable thing about this sentence is the number of nominalizations in it. How many are there? That's right, there are four: *question, discussion, intuition*, and *disclosure.*

It is important to know the following: to produce a sentence that is clear and accurate, you don't **have** to change nominalizations into verbs. It is perfectly acceptable to use nominalizations. **What is NOT acceptable is to NOT know you have them in your sentence,** no matter their function or place, and whether you are Jane Civilian or Joe Academic. And so you'd at least make a list of verbs and then their possible subjects (and these verbs would likely be in active voice), such as the following:

> We question
> We discuss
> We assert (it asserts)
> It discloses (because it seems that tragedy discloses)
> We intuit, or we sense

Note too that as we do this kind of verbal rooting around, we improve our chances of understanding the content of the sentence if at first we'd been unsure of what the author was trying to say.

Also Note: Not every Verb-verb will be used in the new sentence structure, but you want to produce as many verbal building blocks or Lincoln logs as possible to give yourself lots of choices. This will help you to be objective about the condition of that sentence's structure (apart from the words in the structure).

> **Revision Attempts:**
>
> *We want to discuss if intuitions of peace are disclosed only in tragedy.*
>
> *We want to discuss (or decide) if it is only tragedy that discloses intuitions of peace.*
>
> *We will discuss (or examine) the other ways that we can perceive Peace, other than in how tragedy discloses to us the reality of Peace.*

Discussion: I'm not sure I like any of the revisions, and I noticed that I made infinitives when I'd intended to make Verb-verbs. But during revision, you should use the same attitudes that you've been using in drafting—write to see what happens. And write fast. And then, for further help in producing revisions, use FLD with the revisions:

> We want
> >to discuss if
> intuitions of peace are disclosed
> >only in tragedy.
>
> We want
> >to discuss if
> it is
> >only tragedy
> that discloses
> >intuitions of peace.
>
> We will examine
> >the other ways that
> we can perceive
> >Peace, other than how
> tragedy discloses
> >to us the reality of Peace.

One final point: Students who are not confident with their vocabulary often assume that they need a bigger vocabulary to write—or read—at the college level, but they are mistaken. They need only identify the kinds of words they are reading (such as infinitives and nominalizations) and then revise in the light of reader expectations.

Revising Your Own Writing

The following is a sentence I wrote in a previous draft of this chapter:

> *I would submit that a key critical thinking experience that students should practice early and often in their academic careers and after they get into the outside world involves becoming sensitive to what images are triggered by the words they use.*

Notice that the sentence is grammatically correct, but you also get a sense that there is something "off" about it, that it takes a long time to get to its point. Before you understood the Principles of Reader Expectations and before you knew the vocabulary of PRE, you'd likely describe the sentence as "wordy." But now, or soon enough, you will be able to describe why the sentence is wordy, or seems to hang together too loosely. Here is the basic issue with this sentence: The main verb seems to be dozens of words away from its subject, and both readerships (civilian and academic) like the verb to be near the subject.

This is what the sentence looks like in FLD form:

I would submit
   that a key critical thinking
experience that students should practice early and often in their
academic careers
           and after they
             get
             into
             the
             outside
             world
             involves
    becoming sensitive to what
  images are triggered
    by the words
 they use.

Comments: Notice that the second main verb—*involves*—is several words (to be specific, 19 words) away from its subject, and I dramatize that distance by stacking words DOWN when the flush-left line ends on the right and I still have not written down the main subject's verb. This method really emphasizes how far the verb is from its subject.

Another thing to note is that the verbs are near their subjects in all the other SV combinations, which is what both readerships prefer for SV locations. Notice, too, that there are two secondary SV combinations between *involves* and its subject, *experience*.

Also note that the subject is a nominalization, a noun that could be a verb (as in the sentence, *I experience joy when I flush left sentences and see their saggy-sorry structure!*).

Revision Thoughts:

1. First, you would want to put that verb (*involves*) close to its subject, but you might also want to not use *experience* as a subject.

2. Second, you would look at the sequence of actions being described in the sentence. Notice that the actions described in the secondary SV combinations occur before students have that "experience." What is it that students are supposed to practice early? The answer is in the third SV combination: Students are supposed to practice being sensitive to the way images are triggered in their minds by the words they use.

3. Third, expect to come up with several revisions, some not good, but write fast in order to get past the icky stuff quickly.

4. These revisions constitute the "stepping stones" to the final draft.

Here is a revision of the sentence that describes the actions in the sequence that they happen:

I would submit that when students have practiced becoming sensitive to what images are triggered in their minds by the words they encounter, they will have a key critical thinking tool that they can use even outside of the academic world.

Note: I'm not sure if the sentence is as good as it "feels," so a way to get critical distance on it is to use FLD:

I would submit
    that when
students have practiced
    becoming sensitive to what
images are triggered
    in their minds by the words
they encounter,
they will have
    a key critical thinking tool that
they can use
    even outside of the academic world.

As I used FLD with that sentence, my brain gave me another way to word the revision, and here is its flush-left form (note how it differs from the first revision):

I would submit
    that when
students have practiced
    becoming sensitive to the way that
words trigger
    images in *their mind,*
they will have
    a key critical thinking tool that
they can use
    even outside of the academic world.

And then as I flushed that sentence left, another version came to mind:

I would submit
    that when
students *have become*
    sensitive to the way that
words trigger
    images in their mind,
they will have
    a key critical thinking tool that
they can use
    even outside of the academic world.

Note: In all cases, I have made sure that all the verbs are near their subjects, nestled up to them like a fiancée next to her spouse while they drive down the verbal highway of communication.

Making Flush-Left Diagraming Part of Your Revision Activity

- Treat FLD as an autopsy of a sentence: It helps you see the regulatory systems within the body of the sentence.
- Then you can "revive" the sentence by drawing up a revision on the right side of the page.

Here is a sentence from Whitehead's *Adventures of Ideas* (p. 114):

Now it is the beginning of wisdom to understand that social life is founded on routine.

FLUSH-LEFT FORM:

Now

it is

the beginning of wisdom to understand that social

life is founded

on routine.

Quantify the elements in the sentence:

# of words: 16

# of SV combos: 2

# of AVV: 0

# of PVV: 1

# of equal sign verbs: 1

# of people S: 0

of "thing" S: 1

of pronoun S: 1

Infinitives in sentence: *to understand*

Nominalizations in sentence: *beginning*

Plans for revision: will make *to understand* a verb, refer to people; make *beginning* a verb

WRITE DOWN REVISION IDEAS ON THE RIGHT SIDE OF THE PAGE:

Now

it is ⟨Now, we begin to have wisdom when we understand that social life is founded on routine.⟩

the beginning of wisdom to understand that

social life is founded

on routine.

REVISED SENTENCE IN FLUSH-LEFT FORM:

Now,

we begin

to have wisdom when

we understand

that social

life is founded

on routine.

Quantification:

>   # of words: 16
>
>   # of SV combos: 3
>
>   # of AVV: 2
>
>   # of PVV: 1
>
>   # of equal sign verbs: 0
>
>   # of people S: 2
>
>   # of "thing" S: 1
>
>   # of pronoun S:
>
>   Infinitives in sentence: to have
>
>   Nominalizations in sentence:
>
>   Other remarks:
>
>   Plans for revision:

Another sentence by Whitehead (p. 114):

But there are limits to routine, and it is for the discernment of these limits and for the provision of the consequent action, that foresight is required.

FLUSH-LEFT FORM

>   But

there are

>   limits to routine, and

it is

>   for the discernment of these limits and for the provision of the consequent action, that

foresight is required.

Quantification:

>   # of words: 16
>
>   # of SV combos: 3
>
>   # of AVV: 2
>
>   # of PVV: 1
>
>   # of equal sign verbs: 0
>
>   # of people S: 2
>
>   # of "thing" S: 1
>
>   # of pronoun S:
>
>   Infinitives in sentence: *to have*
>
>   Nominalizations in sentence:
>
>   Other remarks:
>
>   Plans for revision: nominalizations will be changed into verb-verbs—maybe infinitives... foresight predicts!

FLUSH-LEFT FORM WITH REVISION ON RIGHT SIDE:

But

there are

<But routine has its limits, and we require foresight so
that we can discern the limits of routine and so we
can anticipate what we need as we act differently from that
routine. [*Now, as I look at this, I wonder if I can start with
a subordinate conjunction:* Because routine has its limits,
we can discern those limits and we act differently from that
routine, though this require that we have foresight.]>

limits to routine, and

it is

for the discernment of these limits and for the provision of the consequent
action, that

foresight is required.

Analysis: Whoa! It occurred to me just now that the struggles students have with learning this stuff in my class were partly due to the routines that they'd developed before coming to college.

THE REVISED SENTENCE:

*But routine has its limits, and we require foresight so that we can discern the limits
of routine and so we can anticipate what we need as we act differently from that
routine.*

REVISED SENTENCE IN FLUSH-LEFT FORM:

But

routine has

its limits, and

we require

foresight so that

we can discern

the limits of routine and so

we can anticipate

what

we need

as

we act

differently from that routine.

FLUSH-LEFT FORM OF SECOND REVISION:

Because
routine has
its limits,
we can discern
those limits and so
we act
differently from that routine, though
this requires
that
we have foresight. ← Note: I put at the end the idea Whitehead had ended with. ☺

The 10-Step Sentence Revision Process

To recap, here is the sequence of revision activities that you might want to do when you find a sentence that the readership you have in mind would like you to revise.

1. Write down the ORIGINAL SENTENCE.

2. Use FLUSH-LEFT DIAGRAMMING on that sentence.

3. Complete the QUANTIFICATION of that sentence or passage.

4. Note COMMENTS on the sentence's features, remarkable things about it, and/or some ideas about how you will revise it.

5. COPY/PASTE the FLD from step 2 AGAIN and give your REVISION on the right side of the FLD.

6. Copy the NEW VERSION, paste it below step 5, and put into prose form.

7. Then use FLD on the NEW VERSION.

8. Do a QUANTIFICATION analysis.

9. Make COMMENTS about the revision.

10. Do another round of revision if necessary, following steps 5–9.

Analyzing Sentences for PRE as a Global Revision Activity

Most handbooks on writing suggest that when you start revising a draft, you look at "global" issues, beginning with the examination of the organization of the entire paper, then moving on to paragraph content and structure, then the word choices in sentences, and finally editing for grammar and such and proofreading. I would like to suggest here that before you do any global revising of this kind, revise sentences for their PRE observance (in the light of the specific audience you are addressing). After all, the PRE are not concerned with the grammar of the sentence, but with the relationships of the parts of the sentence, in the light of reader preferences. This will be especially evident when we learn about analyzing a paragraph for its observance of PRE.

The third thread is present, no matter the grammar or the rhetoric, and in that way it is a global concern. So before you look at the kinds of content in a paragraph, look at the PRE of the sentences.

It is often suggested that you shouldn't look at sentence features in this stage of revision because you might throw out a sentence if its content doesn't fit the paragraph. This is also true in the light of PRE: When you identify a sentence that doesn't conform to location or identity PRE and then revise it, you get images triggered in your head that had not been there before, and those images can help you see features of the topic that had been hidden from you. Then you might write more sentences that become content for the paragraph. All of this occurs just by looking at sentence PRE!

For example, when you replace an equal sign verb with a verb that conveys action (whether in passive voice or active voice), you likely will experience new intellectual growth. An equal sign verb will not trigger any images in your mind, but an action verb will trigger images, and if you have also come up with a subject, you will have two images now in your mind, images that could spotlight or illuminate aspects of your topic that had been in the dark until then. Such revisions of sentences constitute adult-level engagement with words, whether the writer is a civilian or an academic.

Conclusion

I hope that this chapter has helped you learn to read academic texts. A key lesson here is that an **academic text might not be written at the adult level of understanding, as the author might not have yet examined the word–image dynamic, might not be using metaphors consciously and deliberately, and might not use PRE to revise.** You, though, awesome college student, can know the preferences of the civilian and of the academic, and can write for either audience, and without much fatigue in the completion of the challenge, because YOU have a CLEW!

NAME: .... CLASS HOUR: .... DATE: ....

Rewrite these sentences so passive-voice verbs are now active-voice verbs. Write each revision below the original sentence.

1. When trade routes **were created,** more jobs **were invented**.

2. Jesus **is portrayed** in the Gospels as being a pious Jew.

3. Grief **will always be produced** by civilization.

4. An antidote **is being developed** by civilization right now to assuage this grief.

5. Cities **were constructed** by people, but without much forethought.

6. Material once stretched over two or three paragraphs might be condensed into one.

7. Entire paragraphs might be re-arranged.

8. Even the content may change, sometimes dramatically, for the process of writing stimulates thought.

Sentence Revision Part 2: AVV to PVV

Rewrite these sentences so all active-voice verbs are now passive-voice verbs. NOTE: Expect sentences to have more words and to be wordy—that's OK. The bold words in each sentence should be the new subject in the revision.

1. Our economic downturn is producing **lots of anxiety** in people.

2. We consider **noise and busyness** as hallmarks of commercial civilization.

3. The university should develop a **list of foundational perceptions** that faculty could agree on.

4. After we understand that there is **a subjective element in objectivity**, we will think realistically. [Also: Can you change the second verb to a PVV? Try it!]

Revising Whitehead Sentences: Part 1

NAME: .... CLASS HOUR: .... DATE: ....

Here is a sentence by Whitehead (from *Adventures of Ideas,* p. 209). See if you can revise it to meet civilian preferences for subject and verb identities.

I suggest that the development of systematic theology should be accompanied by a critical understanding of the relation of linguistic expression to our deepest and most persistent intuitions.

FLUSH-LEFT DIAGRAM:

QUANTIFICATION:

# of words:

# of SV combos:

# of AVV:

# of PVV:

# of equal sign verbs:

# of people S:

of "thing" S:

of pronoun S:

Infinitives in sentence:

Nominalizations in sentence:

Other remarks:

Plans for revision:

Revision:

FLUSH-LEFT DIAGRAM OF REVISION:

QUANTIFICATION:

# of words:

# of SV combos:

# of AVV:

# of PVV:

# of equal sign verbs:

# of people S:

of "thing" S:

of pronoun S:

Infinitives in sentence:

Nominalizations in sentence:

Assess revision:

Perhaps write another revision:

Revising Whitehead Sentences: Part 2

Here is a sentence by Whitehead (from *Adventures of Ideas,* p. 376). See if you can revise it to meet civilian preferences for subject and verb identities.

> *The analysis of the various strands of relativity is the analysis of the social structure of the Universe, as in this epoch.*

FLUSH-LEFT DIAGRAM:

QUANTIFICATION:

# of words:

# of SV combos:

# of AVV:

# of PVV:

# of equal sign verbs:

# of people S:

of "thing" S:

of pronoun S:

Infinitives in sentence:

Nominalizations in sentence:

Other remarks:

Plans for revision:

Revision:

FLUSH-LEFT DIAGRAM OF REVISION:

QUANTIFICATION:

# of words:

# of SV combos:

# of AVV:

# of PVV:

# of equal sign verbs:

# of people S:

of "thing" S:

of pronoun S:

Infinitives in sentence:

Nominalizations in sentence:

Assess revision:

Perhaps write another revision:

NAME: .... CLASS HOUR: .... DATE: ....

Here is a sentence by Whitehead (from *Adventures of Ideas,* p. 242). See if you can revise it to meet civilian preferences for subject and verb identities.

> *Our perception of the geometrical order of the Universe brings with it the denial of the restrictions of inheritance to mere personal order.*

FLUSH-LEFT DIAGRAM:

QUANTIFICATION:

# of words:

# of SV combos:

# of AVV:

# of PVV:

# of equal sign verbs:

# of people S:

of "thing" S:

of pronoun S:

Infinitives in sentence:

Nominalizations in sentence:

Other remarks:

Plans for revision:

Revision:

FLUSH-LEFT DIAGRAM OF REVISION:

QUANTIFICATION:

# of words:

# of SV combos:

# of AVV:

# of PVV:

# of equal sign verbs:

# of people S:

of "thing" S:

of pronoun S:

Infinitives in sentence:

Nominalizations in sentence:

Assess revision:

Perhaps write another revision:

Secondary and Main SV Combos

NAME: .... CLASS HOUR: .... DATE: ....

Identify the secondary SV combos in the following sentences, and then "extract" them to make them main SVs. You will likely need to use subordinate conjunctions in the revised sentences. Then use FLD on each revision. NOTE: Underline the secondary SV combos before revising.

Example:

Adults <u>who do not look</u> at the images triggered by words will have a hard time thinking critically.

Flush-left diagram:

Adults who do not look at the images triggered by words will have

a hard time thinking critically.

Revision with a subordinate conjunction (*if*):

If adults do not examine the images that are triggered by words in their minds, they will have a hard time thinking critically.

Flushed-left diagram:

If

adults do not examine

the images

that are triggered

by words in their minds,

they will have

a hard time thinking critically.

1. What I wanted to say was that I like reading and writing.

2. Those who like to play with fire tend to burn themselves out quirkily.

3. We who read with a CLEW will see images popping out of the words we read on the page.

4. An integral part that ensures the integrity of this Truth is the ability to keep it as a written record.

5. In my opinion, what Koch is trying to make us understand is that we should open our mind and think outside the box when we think of something.

6. One of the first points that Frye explains on what it is like to be a thinker is his comparison of students to mature thinkers.

7. Another thing Frye talks about is unintelligibility.

Location PRE: Main Verbs and Subjects

NAME: .... CLASS HOUR: .... DATE: ....

Revise each of the following sentences so that the main verb is very close to its subject. Expect to create a few to several new SV combos for each revision.

1. Verbally training someone on room set up and handing down verbally and through notes (written or typed in email) the way that teachers have done and are to do duties at ECNS has worked in the past but it is clear that it is no longer the best way based on misunderstandings and poor communication.

1.

2. We will need to understand that this external acceleration of the pace of change—as evident in many ways, but just for exposition purposes, we will refer to the quick outmodedness of computer levels—will beckon or require that the people in commercial civilization be able to develop a mode of intellectual machinations that also has an ability to accelerate the pace of change, intellectually speaking.

2.

3. Time, that albatross on the conscience of biology's 2nd level of consciousness, that stranger that seems to both mock and admire us, offers a hand of help – and even solicitude – if we but have the right disposition.

   (from

3.

4. Applying the PRE to my other reading assignments by noticing the subject and verb being in the right spot in a sentence has helped me in my writing.

4.

5. Running every day for a couple miles by using the dog for a running mate and barking at him like I'm a dog, too, has proven to be not so helpful.

5.

Verb Revision

Circle two words in each sentence that could become verbs and revise the sentence so they are used as verbs.

TWO PURPOSES: You will see that vocabulary growth occurs with words you already have, and you will get experience in the messiness of revision—it's a time of experimentation, trial and error. This experience with words can lead you to see aspects of your topic that you had not seen before.

NOTE: Use subordinate conjunctions in your revisions when possible.

1. The process that liberal education wants us to embrace for producing acclaimed critical thinking demonstrations allows for messiness of expression in one's early work.

2. Over the time that I've used PRE to analyze texts that college students read, I've come to distinguish two types of readers: You have the civilian reader and the academic (or college) reader.

3. It is important to know that these are features of the sentence that are NOT related to grammar or rhetorical choices.

4. In addition, it is important to know that both the civilian and the academic reader share the SAME expectations (or preferences) about the LOCATION of subjects and verbs.

5. When I understood these concepts from Joseph Williams, I realized that I had a very practical way to explain WHY a sentence or a paragraph doesn't seem to have focus (and why it does).

6. The idea of the exercise is to generate an entire list of words with this process in a short amount of time.

7. The goal of this exercise is to add another tool to facilitate the exploration of the ocean of words.

Sentence Revision: Traction

NAME: .... CLASS HOUR: .... DATE: ....

The following sentences don't get much traction in a civilian reader's mind. Revise them so that the SV combos in each sentence are like claws that grab the reader's attention and won't let the reader take his or her eyes off the text.

Revise with attention to these aspects:

- infinitives
- nominalizations
- use of PVV when it is easily could be AVV
- lack of action verbs
- lack of actor/subjects
- lack of people subjects

NOTE: Remember that subordinate conjunctions can help you produce a verb-verb.

1. Thinking must be carefully and consistently used in order to gain growth and maturity.

2. Stafford introduces to writers that having the willingness to fail will allow them to write down any thought that occurs to them.

3. Errors will occur in the process of writing with the acceptation of failing, but those failures can be fixed during the revision stage.

4. Thinking articulately helps a person to be accurate with the words he or she chooses.

5. Knowing that it is never too late to change your perspective toward writing has helped me the most.

6. Slowly committing to writing instead of being afraid that I might make a mistake has helped me to write.

7. It is a common struggle translating ideas into words.

8. Having known that there are no right words wrapped around an idea, it helps us become more creative in our writing.

9. This statement is proven in every piece of work we produce that is not one of articulateness but of immaturity.

10. These two essays have been a motivation to help me improve my thinking, reading and writing skills.

11. It was a very educational development for me, as I had very little knowledge of formal writing when I started college.

CHAPTER 8

The Phenomena of Paragraphs

Goals:

- Understand the PRE for paragraphs, along with the concepts of contracts, paragraph elements, and old-to-new expectations.
- Learn a process for analysis of paragraph structure.
- Learn a better way to understand why a paragraph has coherence and cohesion, apart from the content of the paragraph.

Outcomes:

- Have the ability to analyze a paragraph to perceive its observance or violation of reader preferences for the structure of a paragraph.
- Have the ability to use the tools of PRE to understand why a text's paragraph gets traction in the reader's mind or why it lacks that trait.
- Have the ability to revise text to ensure it meets reader preferences at the paragraph level.

Terms to Know:

- Contract
- Character
- Concept
- Significance

Familiar information

New information

Fragging – or fracturing – a paragraph

Principles of Reader Expectations Regarding Paragraphs

In this chapter, we will further discuss the Principles of Reader Expectations (PRE) regarding paragraphs, which are as follows:

1. Both readerships (civilian and academic) expect a paragraph to begin with a contract, also referred to as a topic sentence. I call the topic sentence the "contract."

2. Both readerships expect each sentence after the contract to begin with familiar information before that sentence gives new information.

3. Both readerships understand that this familiar information often comes from one of the three elements of the contract, although the familiar information could come from earlier paragraphs or the general topic, or from the new information in the sentence that immediately precedes it.

4. Both readerships expect that new information at the end of the sentence to be significant.

5. Both expect that, as a whole, the beginnings of sentences in a paragraph will refer to a limited but related set of topical subjects.

6. Furthermore, both readerships expect the latter parts of sentences to contain information pertaining to a limited but related set of topics.

A writing teacher once wrote in her handbook on writing the following about how to revise paragraphs: "Many of us resist global revision because we find it difficult to distance ourselves from a draft. We tend to review our work from our own, not from the audience's perspective." In addition, she suggests we get distance by putting the draft away for an hour or overnight. Then she notes, "Play the role of your audience as you read. Mark any places where your readers are likely to be confused, misled, or annoyed; look too for sentences and paragraphs that are not likely to persuade" (Diane Hacker, *The Bedford Handbook, 5th Ed., p. 43*).

But, I would ask, what is the basis of deciding that something is confusing, misleading, or annoying to a reader? The concept of the Principles of Reader Expectations (PRE) can help with this greatly, and because of PRE you can begin to revise as soon as you finish a draft.

Identifying the Contract

Just as we have seen that we can identify a structure in a sentence that is separate from the specific words that are embedded in that structure, so we can do the same for a paragraph. And just as we are not looking at the grammar of the sentence when identifying its structure, the same holds true for the paragraph.

On the inside front cover of this book, you will see a diagram of the paragraph's structure. Like the sentence, it also consists of two parts—in this case, the contract and the development.

I call the topic sentence (which ordinarily begins the paragraph) a **contract** for two reasons: (1) a contract can be more than one sentence long, and (2) the term *contract* reinforces the communication event going on between writer and reader—as writer, you are saying that this paragraph will focus on this particular topic.

The contract, then, is a general statement of the paragraph's focus, but we can also identify three specific aspects of the contract:

- a character,
- a concept, and
- the significance of the two.

After we identify the contract, we then expect each sentence that follows the contract in the paragraph to begin with information familiar to the reader, and often that information will come from the contract, although it could come from earlier paragraphs. Also, once new information is given, it is then "old" information and it could begin the next sentence. (This chain linkage is acceptable on occasion, but not for an extended text).

The diagram from the inside front cover is reproduced here to reinforce this element of the structure of the paragraph:

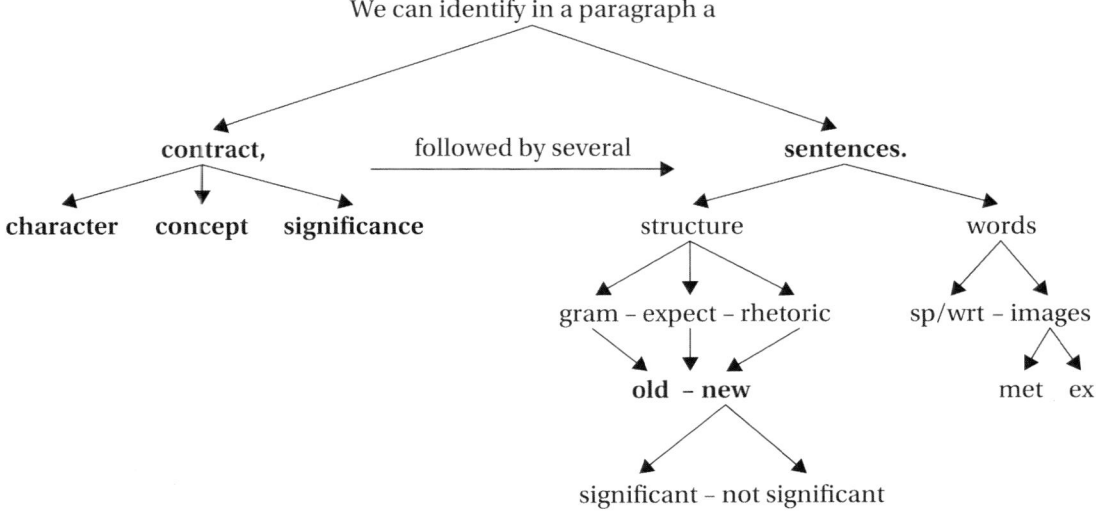

We really cannot know for sure where the contract ends until we have read and studied the paragraph. And a key way to determine the end of the contract is to note when the level of generality becomes more detailed.

So, for example, read the following text, and determine where the level of generality changes:

> He thought that his writing skills improved greatly after he mastered the Principles of Clear Writing from a book by Joseph Williams titled Style. These principles didn't help him with vocabulary or grammar, but they helped him see that any clear sentence must have a certain structure to it, regardless of the specific words in the sentence or passage. Furthermore, Williams pointed out that these principles amount to expectations that readers have when they approach a verbal text. In that regard, he also saw how these principles helped him read through a passage quickly and effectively. And then he felt that the tremendous thing about these principles was that once anyone came to understand how to use them, these principles could even help one think more clearly and deeply.

Note: The level of detail in the sentences shifts with the second sentence. The second sentence describes features of those principles. You can then identify (as a working hypothesis) that the **character** is the student, the **concept** is the principles, and the **significance** involves how they helped him.

Observing the Old-to-New Principle

There is a second great principle or preference involved with the organization of the paragraph, and this deals with the sentences that follow the contract, the sentences that constitute the body of the paragraph. In each sentence that makes up the paragraph, readers prefer that it begin with information that is familiar and then moves to new information only after that point. That familiar information is likely to come from one of the three elements in the contract, although it could come from earlier paragraphs. If each sentence after the contract follows the old-to-new principle, the paragraph has coherence and cohesion. If the paragraph seems to not get traction in the reader's mind, it is likely due to the writer not following (in one way or another) the old-to-new principle or expectation.

Now we will use something that is similar to flush left diagramming (FLD) for analysis, but in this case just the beginnings of sentences start the flush-left lines, from the first word to the first main verb (which should usually appear within the first 10 words).

CONTRACT: Character: bold; Concept: underlined; Significance: italicized

He thought that his <u>writing skills improved</u> greatly after *he mastered the Principles of Clear Writing from a book by Joseph Williams titled Style.*

These *principles* didn't help	him with vocabulary or grammar, but they helped him see that any clear sentence must have a certain structure to it, regardless of the specific words in the sentence or passage.
Furthermore, *Williams* pointed out	that these principles amount to expectations that readers have when they approach a verbal text.
In that regard, **he** also saw	how these principles helped him read through a passage quickly and effectively.
And then **he** felt	that the tremendous thing about these principles was that once anyone came to understand how to use them, these principles could even help one think more clearly and deeply.

Analysis: All four sentences begin with words that refer to elements in the contract.

Fragging (or Fracturing) a Paragraph

I've found that fragging, or fracturing, a paragraph, as in this example, allows students to more easily see whether it observes or violates paragraph expectations. To do that, first state what you think is the contract and then list all the sentences below it, each on its own line. Then start each sentence flush left, but after you get to the first main verb, bump the rest of the sentence to the far right. That way, it's easier to see whether familiar information is presented early in each sentence. Additionally, you get a visual of how long each sentence is. When you frag a paragraph, it is then relatively easy to see whether familiar information is given early in the sentence. Indeed, notice this: **The familiar information is often the SUBJECT in the first subject–verb (SV) combination.** Also notice that familiar information can be one word, and everything after that the reader will accept as new information.

Note: In any sentence, where does the familiar information occur? **In almost all situations, the familiar information is the grammatical subject.**

How Images Triggered by Words in the Contract Generate Expectations

Here is another way to think of the organization of the paragraph: The contract contains key words that readers expect will be used in the body of the paragraph. These key words should be repeated, although not slavishly. Certainly the adult reader will understand the need to use synonyms or words whose shades of meaning advance the exposition (whether argumentative or expository) in unexpected directions (and later seem natural enough), but if the writer has an adult-level engagement with words, he or she will know which words are to be repeated in the body of the paragraph and where in each sentence to repeat them. Indeed, for such writers, their intellect even directs their selection of words, so to speak.

Then there is this consideration: These key words (and non-essential words) trigger images in the mind of the reader, and these images generate expectations about what to expect in the sentences that immediately follow the contract. The reader can then use these images to determine if the writer is meeting the expectations that readers have about the coherence and cohesion of a paragraph.

EXAMPLE: Here is a contract written by a student who is applying for a teaching assistantship:

As a teacher I would like to accomplish helping each of my students grow, as a person and as a learner.

Now: Aside from the wordiness of the sentence, what images do those words trigger in your mind? Due to words like *teacher* and *I*, you likely have images of a classroom and a young teacher teaching kids (at least I do). Also, the character, concept, and significance can be identified as follows:

Character: *I*

Concept: *helping students*

Significance: *feels accomplished*

So we would expect words related to the character or concept early in the next sentence. But here is the next sentence:

No one program fits every child.

Note: The writer's point might be valid, but note the following violations of PRE:

1. None of the key words in the contract is found here.

2. The statement is like another contract and it is an evaluation.

3. We expected to read how she'd help students grow.

The writer's third sentence is this:

I want to read and learn to continue to grow professionally so that I can have a better understanding of how students learn, so that I can meet each student's needs.

Note: The content in this third sentence is not closely related to the prior sentence, which itself wasn't closely or overtly linked to the contract. I can see how in her mind she felt she was being coherent, because the word *each* likely triggered the idea of individuality and the claims prominent today that individuality means no common linkages among students. But she needed to examine what words in the first sentence likely triggered images in her readers' minds and at least write a draft with those preferences in mind and then compare it with this rendition and decide which to submit.

Bottom line: The organization of the paragraph can be discerned using two basic principles:

1. The contract, with its three elements
2. Sentences after the contract observing the old-to-new principle in each sentence

Using the Old-to-New Principle as a Diagnostic Tool

The concept of sentences beginning with old information followed by new information can help you detect the nature of paragraphs that don't get any traction in your mind.

For instance, what feeling do you get about this paragraph after reading it?

I began my "refresher course" with the intention of understanding writing theory more, as well as finding techniques for teaching writing. But the reading component in the title of our course-College Reading and Writing, though, was just as interesting to me. At the end of her 1995 essay on the state of composition theory, Karen Spears began the list of introductory practices "that are finding their way into some beginning writing courses" with "Greater emphasis on **reading** to help students understand the posture toward texts that seasoned academics assume" (np). At the end of 2005, I had arrived at this attitude and it provided me with material for a two-day discussion of some of the key essays in our MR.

If you apply the old-to-new principle, you notice that each sentence begins with new information and then is followed by either more new information or old information. For this reason, the paragraph seems choppy or disconnected. Fragging the paragraph shows this more clearly, directly, or obviously.

ANOTHER PARAGRAPH: What feeling do you get about this paragraph after reading it?

> I would also submit that not only should students know about music and art, they should *play* instruments and *produce* works of art. The emotional side of the person's consciousness is affected when practicing a musical instrument. They will find that when they practice an instrument their emotional side is improved. They will see that the practice has not only an intellectual side (caused by knowing theory and seeing its use in understanding what they practice) but they will also see how their emotions are improved, such as confidence that their practice does lead to perfection, even if just of a musical phrase in the music they are learning. The imagination is being developed, too, which also makes their emotions feel better. And then these new experiences (that are emotional in nature) can be used by the student as a metaphor for difficult task in other areas of their lives, areas that require the use or words.

Once again, the principle of old to new shows us that this paragraph feels boring because several of its sentences begin and end with old information. The paragraph seems to be "spinning its wheels."

Example from a Peer-Reviewed Article

Following are two paragraphs from an essay I had published in *English Studies in Canada*, and even after the article was published, I still felt uneasy with the organization of each of these paragraphs. As an example, I will analyze them for their observance of old-to-new expectations—or lack thereof—and show the results of the analysis.

Here are the two paragraphs, preceded by an introductory paragraph:

> In producing a reflection for this centenary of Frye's birth, then, I'd like to just say a couple things about *Fearful Symmetry* as a whole (though I've already produced several drafts in which I tried to do just that!).
>
> First, even though the book is about the poetry of William Blake and what Frye called Blake's "canon," I think it provides incoming college students with a template of the major intellectual issues that they should face in liberal education (but alas, might very well be able to evade). Among these issues are epistemology, hermeneutics, one's understanding and experience of Art. With regards to Art, I ask my classroom students, "Why do you suppose that liberal education has traditionally been divided into ARTS and Sciences?" Such a division

suggests that educated people have found their engagement with the Arts (and the artistic method) to be as important as Science (and the scientific method) in producing important knowledge.

And so it is interesting that the first chapters of *Fearful Symmetry* outline Blake's argument with Locke, and Frye's entire study hangs together with the contrasting of the Lockean and Blakean conception of the mind and their implication. In his explication, Frye not only explains how Art is central to Blake's argument, but he explains how Art links the person to what are called divine creative powers.

Here is my fracturing of the first problematic paragraph. Note the highlighting of the observance of old to new, but also note that I don't repeat words from the contract but from the prior sentences.

First, even though the book is about the poetry of William Blake and what Frye called Blake's "canon," I think it provides incoming college students with a template of the major intellectual **issues** that they should face in liberal education (but alas, might very well be able to evade).

> **Character:** the book
> **Concept:** conveys major intellectual issues
> **Significance:** college students should know

Expectations for next sentence:

Among **these issues** are	epistemology, hermeneutics, one's understanding and experience *of Art*.
With regards to *Art*, I ask	my classroom students, "Why do you suppose that liberal education has traditionally been <u>divided</u> into ARTS and Sciences?"
Such a <u>division</u> suggests that educated	people have found their engagement with the Arts (and the artistic method) to be as important as Science (and the scientific method) in producing important knowledge.

Comment: Notice that what is considered familiar information is familiar because I'd used those words near the end of the prior sentences. This gives the feel of a box-car linkage, which doesn't really help the reader feel that the paragraph has focus. If a paragraph has focus, then all the arrows would be ending up with their pointy tips in the contract (although an earlier element in the essay could also be referred to).

As for revision, I ended up using sentences from the third paragraph of the excerpt presented here. This is what the revised paragraph looks like in "fractured" form:

First, even though the book is about the poetry of William Blake and what Frye called Blake's "canon," I think it provides incoming college students with a template of the major intellectual **issues** that they should face in liberal education (but alas, might very well be able to evade).

Among **these issues** are   epistemology, hermeneutics, one's under-
                                                    standing and experience *of Art*.

As a group, these **issues** help   the students know themselves better, help
                                              them have a deeper engagement with basic
                                              intellectual tools.

Indeed, **the issue** of
epistemology is at the heart   of the structure of the entire book, as
                                          Frye describes Blake's argument with
                                          Locke over their conceptions of the
                                          mind and the implications of their basic
                                          conceptions

Note: Some might say that it isn't good to begin each sentence with the same word—in this case, *issue*. That might be true, and so to ease my worried heart, I'd test out replacement words.

But, moving on, because I had prospected in the third paragraph for "gems" to put into the second paragraph, I now worked on that third paragraph, and found I could use the "gems" from the second paragraph in the third paragraph, and this is what I came up with (in its fractured form):

I think that it is extremely noteworthy that Blake's entire **Argument** constitutes a justification for one half of the traditional basic division of liberal education.

Character: argument? Blake? LE?
Concept: justifies art
Significance: LE is half art

Might I call it his "**Artgument**"? ☺

In any case, because *I've* read some of Blake

ever since I was in music school in the late 1970s, I ask students in my writing class almost every semester, "Why do you suppose that liberal education has traditionally been divided into ARTS and Sciences?"

Such a division suggests that educated people

have found their engagement with the Arts (and the artistic method) to be as important as Science (and the scientific method) in producing important knowledge

Note: As you see, all arrows in this revision also end up in the contract. Sometimes it is fine to begin a sentence with information that was just presented in the prior sentence. We can see examples of that in almost any essay. But, as usual, **the most important thing is that you know that you are violating the expectations or preferences of the reader.** It also appears that for the college student who is concerned about two readerships, the civilian and the academic, both prefer to have paragraphs focused this way.

Here now are my two revised paragraphs together, although I've only included the paragraph that precedes these two and the paragraph that follows them. Still, you can get a sense now of the improved cohesion within the paragraphs and also their relationship with their surrounding sections:

In producing a reflection for this centenary of Frye's birth, then, I'd like to just say a couple things about *Fearful Symmetry* as a whole (though I've already produced several drafts in which I tried to do just that!).

First, even though the book is about the poetry of William Blake and what Frye called Blake's "canon," I think it provides incoming college students with a template of the major intellectual **issues** that they should face in liberal education (but alas, might very well be able to evade). Among **these issues** are epistemology, hermeneutics, one's understanding and experience *of Art*. As a group, these **issues** help the students know themselves better, help them have a deeper engagement with basic intellectual tools. Indeed, **the issue** of epistemology is at the heart of the structure of the entire book, as Frye describes Blake's argument with Locke over their conceptions of the mind and the implications of their basic conceptions.

I think that it is extremely noteworthy that Blake's entire Argument constitutes a justification for one half of the traditional basic division of liberal education. Might I call it his "Artgument"? ☺ In any case, in part because I've read some of Blake since I was in music school in the late 1970s, I ask students in my writing class almost every semester, "Why do you suppose that liberal education has traditionally been divided into ARTS and Sciences?" Such a division suggests that educated people have found their engagement with the Arts (and the artistic method) to be as important as Science (and the scientific method) in producing important knowledge.

And within the context of liberal education, it is startling to read this: "Wisdom consists in the mental war which is art and the mental hunting which is science, and these constitute the eternal life of a Man who is God" (271; see also 71). Frye then clarifies this statement with syllogistic maneuvers which seem to compel assent: "Art is human, but it is also divine because God is creator. Science is human, but it is also divine because God can hardly be the lazy and inert Omniscience which a lazy and inert mind is apt to envisage" (271).

Questions to Ask to Judge Whether a Paragraph Is Structured Effectively

About the PRE structure of the paragraph:

1. How long is the contract? (Notice when the level of generality changes to a deeper level of detail.)

2. What are the character, concept, and significance in the contract?

3. What expectations does the contract set up in the reader's mind as to what will begin the next sentence?

4. Does familiar information begin the next sentence? (That is, does the next sentence meet the expectations generated in the reader's mind by the words in the contract?)

5. Is the familiar information related to the contract elements, or to something else?

6. Do the beginnings of all sentences contain familiar information?

7. As a set, does the familiar information constitute a narrow, related set of topics (one or two topics)?

8. Do the sets of information that end sentences comprise significant information?

Other aspects of the paragraph:

1. What are the structures of these sentences—for example, single independent clauses, compound sentences with dependent and independent clauses, compound independent clauses?

2. What are the rhetorical images triggered by the major words of the sentences?

3. Are the structures of sentences made that way for emotional (rhetorical) impact?

4. Can the images be categorized into contrasting sets of forces, complementary sets, or something else?

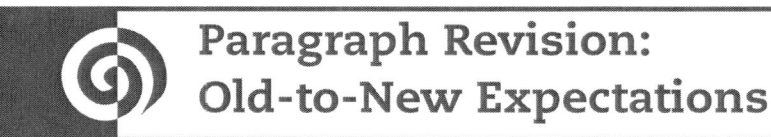

NAME: .... CLASS HOUR: .... DATE: ....

Revise the paragraph on page 182 that seems to be "spinning its wheels" so that it meets the old-to-new expectation. Write the paragraph here and then frag it, drawing arrows from the old information in each sentence to the contract. You can print it on this page, too, if you like.

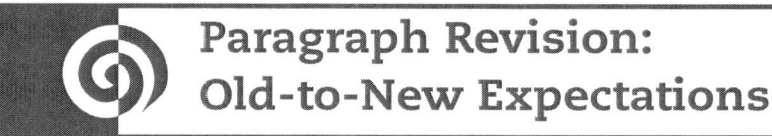
NAME: .... CLASS HOUR: .... DATE: ....

Revise the paragraph on page 181 that seems to be "choppy" so that it meets the old-to-new expectation. Write the paragraph here and then frag it, drawing arrows from the old information in each sentence to the contract. You can print it on this page, too, if you like.

NAME: .... CLASS HOUR: .... DATE: ....

The following paragraph violates reader expectations in regard to having a clear contract and old-to-new observance. Read the paragraph, then work through the activities that follow.

Along with the differences in the authors, there is also a difference between when the narratives seem to be written. It is not known the exact date the Old Testament was written but it is thought to have been recorded between 1440 and 1400 B.C. The Babylonian account of the flood story and the Epic of Gilgamesh is much older. It is believed that the Gilgamesh story was known back in 2000 B.C. However, like the Old Testament the exact date is unknown. The Babylonian version therefore would have been well known before the time of Noah and the Jewish version of the flood. Many researchers believe that the two are based on a true event even farther back in history. (121 words)

1. List all subject–verb combinations and change passive-voice verbs to active-voice verbs.

2. Write a new draft with subjects that are actors (which means all verbs are active-voice verbs). Do not revise the contract yet.

3. Rewrite the contract so that it has actors in the subject position and active-voice verbs.

4. Write the new contract with the new development and revise as needed for flow—that is, to meet old-to-new expectations

Paragraph Revision Part 2: Contract Observance

NAME: .... CLASS HOUR: .... DATE: ....

Rework the paragraph on page 178 written to apply for a teaching assistantship. Follows these steps:

1. Use the first sentence as the contract and make the third sentence the second sentence (drop what had been the second sentence).

2. Revise both sentences so that some of the infinitives and nominalizations are now verb-verbs.

3. Add more content (as you imagine the writer would add, being a teaching major) so that you have a paragraph with seven sentences, of varying lengths.

4. Then frag the paragraph to show how it meets old-to-new expectations.

5. NOTE: As a way to generate ideas for content, examine the images triggered in your mind by the first two sentences.

   a. Write down the images triggered in your mind by the words in the original sentences.

   b. Then see if other images occur to you from the words in your revisions of those sentences.

Write here your final draft of the paragraph, on the other side of the page, put the same paragraph in the fragged or fractured form.

CHAPTER 9

The Research Experience

It might be better if the university confined itself to supplying the historical dimension of its culture. (Northrop Frye, *The Modern Century* 103)

It is clearly one of the unavoidable responsibilities of educated people to show by example that beliefs may be held and examined at the same time. (Northrop Frye, *The Critical Path* 109)

Goals:

- Give students an experience of college-level research that is solely book-based research.

Outcomes:

- Know how to read widely quickly.
- Know how to write annotated bibliographies.
- Know how to use conventions of MLA citation format correctly.

A General Rationale for Research in College

I want to begin this chapter on research by stressing that when college students present an essay based on research (scholarship), that essay should not just be regurgitating what scholars have already opined on the subject. Instead, students are to prepare themselves to join the discussion or conversation. Even if the topic concerns a hot-button social issue, students shouldn't approach the research as an attempt only to find sources that agree with their position.

Considering the experiences you have had with words up to this point in this text, I would conjecture that you might now assume that you will encounter writers who have engaged with words as intimately—and intelligently—as you have.

Of course, often that is not the case. But now, as you read widely in topics for your college courses, you will have the "X-ray" vision that comes with knowing the Principles of Reader Expectations (PRE), and you will know that sometimes it is hard to understand academic texts because:

1. You have yet to learn the specific vocabulary for each college subject.

2. Writers often violate reader preferences about the location of subjects and verbs (even though you know better!).

3. You still need to become familiar with the specialized expectations of academics for subject and verb identities.

I've discussed at length the issue of engaging with academic texts because college student scholarship presumes that the student:

1. Knows the diversity of opinion on a topic.

2. Knows the history behind the issue or topic.

3. Knows the major concepts involved.

4. Knows which experts have given major contributions to understanding the issue or topic.

Sadly, most students do not have that kind of background before writing a "research paper." The particular research project outlined in this chapter seeks to remedy that deficiency.

The first way that we will remedy this deficiency is by noting that if you are doing a research project in college, you should **read widely** on the topic (no matter what your topic is), before you decide which few books (even if it is five) you will use for your presentation. This means that you can't spend a lot of time on each book in the "invention" stage of the reading project. Instead, you will want to skim the contents of the book, and in this chapter I give a more detailed explanation of that process.

Second, you should not think that in your first round of research, you have to understand many of the terms used in these texts that you are encountering for the first time. Instead, you should note the "frequently used terms" that many authors use. This set of terms refers to the concepts and the "fossil record" that all scholars are aware of and that leads them sometimes to arrive at differing conclusions—or to agree that such-and-such theory explains the evidence.

So, expect to start your research with a haze of unclear understanding, but expect that your persistent and methodical contact with this material will lead to a clearer understanding. Even more important, you should feel that your understanding is advancing, which also can be troubling because you will be leaving behind a childhood understanding of complex concepts.

In addition, your approach to this "research reading" should be similar to how you engaged with the essays in the chapter on reading. That kind of critical thinking involves opening up an issue and not closing it down. Expect to come up with distinctions that refresh and liberate your understanding from that simplistic childhood notion to an adult—and enlightened—understanding.

Depending on the topic, you might feel profound "cognitive dissonance," but this is a common feature of critical thinking. You are getting a "critical distance" on the topic through critical thinking, and this is what causes such cognitive dissonance. Just remember that for all you previously knew about this topic, it likely constituted only a spotlight of understanding on the realities of this topic. The information isn't meant to challenge the merits of your beliefs—it is only challenging your understanding of those things. You have to start somewhere, though. So recognize what you have, and expect to engage more deeply in the topic than you'd assumed you could handle. Welcome to liberal education!

The WRC Research Topic: The History of Narratives (and Personalities) That Cultures Have Claimed to be Inspired

I would like you to read widely on the scholarship of the formation of written texts that cultures have called "sacred texts." You will **not** read up on how to understand or interpret that text but instead on the history behind that text. Some of the questions you will be seeking answers to from these scholars are:

- Who wrote the text?
- When did they write the text?
- Why did they write the text?
- What sources did the writers use for their writing?
- Was the text revised?
- Who revised it?
- Why did they revise the text?

Because most of us have grown up in a culture that has given a place of honor to the Bible, I'd like you to read widely on what scholars have determined to be the history of the formation of the Bible—the Bible as a whole, the Old Testament and New Testament, and the individual books in the Bible.

BUT you will also read up on **two other things**:

- Scholarship on the formation of a **non-Christian** text that has been considered sacred
- Biographies (not autobiographies) of important people connected to religion, people like Darwin, Freud, Newton, Copernicus, Marx and others.

My premise is that even if you know a lot about religion, it is likely still just a spotlight on that topic. And your understanding began when you were a child, so it is likely the words about religion from back then still trigger the same images, images that are simplistic, considering the complexity of a topic like religion. This should be evident to you, especially if you are in the late-teenage years or early 20s. To assume when you are in your late teens or early 20s that you have an ultimate understanding of ultimate texts is the height of hubris. That advancing to such levels of understanding radically changes the understanding you brought into college is inevitable and expected. Even if you are totally irreligious, it is likely your spotlight on this significant concern in human society isn't very bright or wide.

Again, the areas of research: There are three basic areas to research:

1. Scholarship on the history of the composition of the Bible and of specific books in the Bible

2. Scholarship about the formation of a non-Christian religion's written text

3. Biographies of important Western personalities, such as Darwin, Newton, and Marx

An Important Distinction to Keep in Mind:
You are NOT reading up on how to **interpret** a text
or how people over the centuries have understood the content of a text.
Instead, you are to read scholars' work on how
they believe a text was created and formed,
and how the **original** writers and audiences likely understood what they were doing.
To repeat:
You will be examining what scholars have concluded
about the formation of texts
—and of significant figures of Western thought—
that cultures have called inspired and sacred.

With regard to the Western sacred text (the Bible), you should look into:

- What scholars say about how the **Bible as a whole** was formed;
- What scholars say about how a **specific book** of the Bible was formed; and
- Whether there is **scholarly consensus** on any of these matters about the formation of these texts.

Key terms you will find: From my own research into the Western sacred text, I have learned that the following terms are found in a lot of the scholarship on the Bible.

With regard to the Old Testament, you can expect to see these terms (or their variants) used:

- J source
- P source
- E source
- D source
- Typology
- Redactor
- Documentary Theory

With regard to the New Testament, you can expect to see these terms:

- Q source (in Gospels)
- Synoptic
- Form criticism
- Textual criticism
- Redaction criticism

All of these terms will likely be found in the index of any book that you are consulting for your research.

Rubrics for the First Three Research Papers

Each of the first three essays will have these features:

1. Each research paper will focus on just one book.

2. The topic of the paper need only cover a few pages in that book (see next section).

3. Each research paper will be on a different text, on a **different** topic.

4. The topics can come from any of the three areas you dipped into.

5. Even though you use just one source, act like you are using several sources and **mention the source name in every paragraph**.

6. In the first paragraph, mention the source's FULL name and the book title.

7. You will need to cite page numbers in every paragraph that uses information from the source.

8. Each essay will quote three sentences, and place the tagline in three different places.

9. No less than 15 percent and no more than 25 percent of the essay will be direct quotations.

10. The length of final draft must be 550–600 words.

11. You will use MLA citation mechanics.

12. Create a title for your essay that has letter play in it (perhaps do a Letter Linkage session on key words from the book you are using) and give us a sense of the content of the essay.

13. Include a bibliography (place five lines after the end of the essay).

Possible ways to limit the focus of the essays: Each paper is to deal with a different book, although each essay need only explain a **section** of that book. For instance:

- You could write on one chapter out of a book, or a section of that chapter.
- You could write on one article out of an anthology, or a section of that article.
- You could write on a concept that is explained in one chapter of a book—for instance, you could explain what the author says about the J source, or the P source.
- You also might want to look in the index for a key term, and if it is treated in several places in the book, examine those pages and write a paper on that topic.

Final summary essay: In the final summary essay, you will describe the differences between your understanding of your topic before you began this research project and your current understanding, after a month of reading and reflection. Use this organization plan:

- Describe your understanding of the topic prior to research—the topic can be as general as "religion" or "religions of the world."
- Say something about the three sources that you used for your papers. Describe them as easy to read or hard to read, and whether they gave you information that you were not aware of (it is hoped). Give a quotation from each source.
- For each quotation, use a verbal tagline, such as: "Merton noted, ..." BUT:
  - Put one tagline at the start of the quotation.
  - Put one within the quotation (usually within the first five or seven words).

- Put one at the end of the quotation.
- And then sum up how you now view the topic AND also describe the important questions about the issue that you think still need to be answered or explored.
- Include a bibliography that is called Works Cited.
- The length should be 700–900 words, or around three pages, plus the Works Cited page.

Note on the sources: YOU CAN ONLY USE BOOKS IN THE ROD LIBRARY. In other words, you cannot use Web sites in your research essays. Indeed, for this particular research project, I will take you to the section of the library that has the books (hundreds of them, if not thousands) that you will be able to use for this project.

I limit students to using these books for a few reasons:

1. These days, most students only use Web sources for their research papers.

2. Books are peer reviewed so you know that they've endured some level of criticism.

3. Books are lightweight and easy to handle.

4. Books allow you to skip easily from the end to the beginning of the text. This is useful because often the writer consciously repeats key images at the end of the book that had also appeared in the beginning of the book.

5. Books tend to be easier on the eyes than the shimmering monitor screen.

6. In the past, students have been impressed to find substantial books easily and quickly.

7. Indeed, I'd submit that the elements for constructing answers to the key questions of modern people are in the library, in books, and "all" we need to do is take the time to search and identify those elements, then discuss with others the best verbal structure to convey answers (or responses) to our key questions.

A Process for Skimming Books

Because you will have a limited amount of time to read enough books before the Annotated Bibliography is due, let me again describe the kind of reading process, covered earlier in the book, that will take 15 minutes per book and give you a good sense of what is in that book. Also, expect to come across good sources or sections by accident. This is called "serendipity," and scholars expect this to happen as they engage with the written products of other engaged minds.

First, examine the TABLE OF CONTENTS (TOC).

- The table of contents is an outline of the book.
- It will give you a sense of the key themes or topics that are covered in the book.
- It is like the mental structure in the mind of the writer.
- You can think of your work as installing that outline, that structure of understanding, into your own mind.
- Also, as you dip into the book, you might want to refer back to the TOC to see where that content fits in the overall scheme of the book.

Second, look in the INDEX in the back of the book.

- Skim the index for your key words.
- Be aware that you might come across synonyms for the key words you are looking for.
- Also see what words or people are used a lot in the book.
  - You can detect this by the number of page numbers after each term in the index.
  - The more numbers, the more discussion is given to that term or person.

Third, DIP into the book by using key words from the index.

- You could also dip into the book by using key words from the table of contents.
- Skim the few pages noted in the TOC or index to get a sense of writing style and perhaps some content.

Fourth, read the INTRODUCTION.

- The introduction is often the last thing the author writes, but it is placed first in the book.
- The writer sums up his or her thesis and arguments in the introduction.
- Often you'll find summaries of each of the chapters.
- You'll also find explanations of the author's purpose and perhaps evidence of any biases.

DON'T DO THIS OVERVIEW TOO QUICKLY, but limit yourself to 15 minutes for each book. By then you have a sense of what is in the book, enough to write an annotation. Also, as you notice that scholars use many of the same historical documents and agreed-upon concepts, you will become familiar with the issues they are dealing with. You'll notice which concepts are backed with scholarly consensus and which concepts are still being debated.

THE KINDS OF NOTES YOU TAKE:

You are encouraged to take three levels of notes:

1. First, you take notes as if you were writing a multi-source research paper and so you need notes that answer those reporter's questions. (but of course, your research papers will each be on just one book).

2. Then you take some notes for the annotation. These would involve what the entire book covers – and you get info about that from the table of contents and the general ease of reading the text. Note: you would not use notes from your first level of notes in the annotation, except very generally.

3. Then I'd suggest you write about how the information is challenging your prior understanding of the topic, and write about your experience of doing this level of research, and perhaps about the use of books for research.

Annotated Bibliography

An Annotated Bibliography consists of a bibliography followed by a brief summary of the contents of the source. A sample follows. For this Annotated Bibliography, you will use MLA citation format, which lists sources alphabetically, by each author's last name.

Every bibliography should look like the following sample below. NOTE: The first line of a citation is flush left and all other lines are indented. Single space the lines. Skip a line after the bibliography. Tab the entire annotation so it is all indented one tab. Then skip a line between entries. Here is my sample:

Williams, Joseph. *Style: The Basics of Clarity and Grace*. 3rd ed. New York: Longman, 2003.

Williams provides a lot of valuable advice on how to improve one's writing style and he does this in a humorous way. I will use this book when explaining the differences between rules and guidelines.

Grade scale (assuming MLA format is used correctly):

A = 25 sources

B = 20 sources

C = 15 sources

Sample Essay

Following is an example of a single-book essay that focuses on one aspect of the history of the formation of the Old Testament. Things to notice as you read:

1. The author's name is mentioned in each paragraph.

2. The author's name is mentioned before the first page number is cited.

3. The tagline appears in three different places.

Basing the Bible's Beginnings in Babylonia

In *A History of the Bible: An Introduction to the Historical Method*, by Dr. Fred Bratton, professor of biblical history at Duke, we read of the ways that the Old Testament writers seemed to use ancient Babylonian documents. Bratten compared thousands of clay tablets that had been found in the ancient library of Anshubanipul and these tablets were inscribed with Babylonian legends (26). The author translates a lot of these texts and then shows that or suggests that the writers of the Old Testament seemed to use them to convey their own religious take on things.

The book of Genesis, says Bratton, gives us the clearest examples of the Hebrew writing using Babylonian myths. For instance, Bratton claims that the story of Noah and the flood was an adaptation of the the Babylonian flood legend that is found in the Gilgamesh Epic. (27). He provides an excerpt from the Gilgamesh Epic that describes the deluge. As with the Hebrew tale, a protagonist is instructed to build an ark and fill it with his family and animals. At the end of the storm, both texts tell of the release of three birds to find dry land. Bratton concludes, "the Hebrew account is dependent on the Babylonian or that both are versions of an earlier original" (29). The Bible's creation story of the earth and heavens by God likely originated from the Babylonian battle between Tiamat and Marduk, notes Bratton. After slaying Tiamat, the representation of chaos, the supreme deity Marduk fixed her body as the firmament, dividing the earth and the heavens, thereby creating order (30). Bratton does offer a note of caution, here though. "The Genesis account," he admits, "may be dependent to some extent on the older Babylonian forms but the advanced religious genius of the Hebrews produced a loftier and vastly more dignified description of what they, at least, thought was the beginning of the world" (31). We should note that the Hebrew writer changed the polytheism of the Babylonian view into the monotheism of the Hebraic religion.

We can even see connections between the Babylonian accounts and the Bible outside the book of Genesis. For example, the book of Exodus and the Hammurabi Code of Babylonia provide an interesting example. "It would not be surprising to find considerable dependence of the Old Testament laws on the Hammurabi Code," Bratton suggests (33). He adds, "Indeed, in the case of some fifty articles in the so-called

Mosaic laws the identity is practically verbatim" (33). Likewise, in the book of Job, the trials of Job mirror the suffering of Tabu-utul-bel in its Babylonian counterpart (36).

Several trends can be observed in the transition of these stories into the Bible. The first, as mentioned, is the shift towards monotheism. "As in other Hebrew-Babylonian comparison, the Babylonian account reveals a more polytheistic and less ethical atmosphere than the Hebrew," Bratton observes (29). This ethical atmosphere may have resulted from the need for the Hebrew to stress the importance of good and evil, and the consequences of one's actions. This conscientiousness is not emphasized in the Babylonian texts. In comparing the Hebrew and Babylonian accounts, the parallels point to the origins of the Bible, but the differences provide an illustration of how these legends have evolved to give birth to a new religion.

Works Cited

Bratton, Fred Gladstone. *A History of the Bible: An Introduction to the Historical Method.* Boston: Beacon Press, 1959.

Justification for Focusing on the Historical Record

This assignment arises from my experience of student responses to the Stephen Jay Gould essay I used to have them read. Most responses ended with the claim that there will never be a resolution between science and religion over the issues of evolution and the Bible. But it has been my experience that as I've developed my literacy skills, I've come to feel that the perspectives of liberal education will help us all see the way out of this impasse. But the solution isn't just in having a "balanced" view; it also requires that we have the right proportions of assumptions and perspectives, activities and goals.

It seems to me that liberal education's many intellectual activities can be reduced to three perspectives, or consciousnesses: **the scientific, the historical, and the literary** (I treated this claim in the chapter on assumptions). When students enter college, they have an adequate grasp of the scientific, less so of the historical, and a rather inadequate understanding of the literary. But this is OK. You have to start somewhere! What this book has taught so far is that the critical thinking process accepts present conditions and then offers you devices for being realistic about the quality of those conditions. Also, the critical thinking process gives you tools to advance your understanding, and this process is perfect because it allows messiness and confusion of thought in the early stages of a critical thinking project, whether you are doing it with writing or reading.

But **most students' knowledge of history is somewhat inadequate,** and it is this condition that I want students to address in this research project. That is why the emphasis isn't on how to interpret a text that their culture has called sacred or inspired. Instead, the emphasis is on knowing what scholars say is the history of the formation of those texts.

This is an area of knowledge that is complex, and students have not known of this history until now for that reason. It's been my experience that a little knowledge of history has radical effects on a whole array of assumptions and presumptions. For some students—whether coming into the project as theists or atheists—the experiences can be traumatic. And I want to emphasize that even the atheists have much to learn.

For the 19- or 20-year-old believer or skeptic to assume that he or she has an ultimate understanding of ultimate things is, as mentioned, hubris. But at the same time, students know they have powerful critical thinking tools and know that their potency is only as good as the level of engagement with which they approach and use words. And the early activities in this book are meant to acquaint you with powers of the word that you hadn't suspected were in you. (Indeed, I wonder if an adult-level engagement with words produces an ultimate engagement with and understanding of things that are conveyed to us via words?)

Again, we are dealing with words, but with words that are used for social questions, such as why we are here, why things are the way that they are. You were taught answers to these questions in childhood, and for the most part you were taught the key words that survive critical scrutiny. But you now realize that the images linked to those words are also from childhood, and they are likely inadequate to adult thinking on the topic. In addition, coming into college, you likely did not have an adult – or ultimate – understanding of these things called ultimate. How could you? And so in this project you will read up on the history behind the formation of these texts, not to decide on how to interpret the texts (which was Gould's focus) but to know what scholars are saying about the history behind the formation of the texts that cultures call sacred.

A Student Objection to the Focus of This Research Project and My Response

I often ask students to describe on the back of the essay they are submitting how they felt while reading up on what scholars said about the formation of the Bible. One student wrote that my research project might make students face things that they are not wanting to take so seriously or that will change their beliefs. Others have voiced similar thoughts, and I have thought often about this kind of reaction to the research topic. But for this particular remark, I wrote down the following thoughts:

1. First, students are not having their beliefs changed as much as they are changing the images triggered by key words that they were taught in childhood.

2. This kind of challenging can't be a bad thing if we want to attain adult and childlike thinking (childlike referring to unbiased and pure vision, or understanding).

3. Second, oh well [I wrote], at least they aren't putting their **physical** bodies on the line for the sake of liberty.

4. Instead, they should feel fortunate to be on a campus that lets students examine the meaning of liberty without putting their physical bodies on the line.

5. They only put their **psychical** bodies on the line, their bodies of assumptions about what constitutes the literal truth of the those texts that society has told them are sacred, or inspired. In addition, they are examining those things that they already assume they know fully well.

6. Liberal education asks students—and faculty—to get a critical distance on the things they love and to come to doubt (for a season) that they have the ultimate understanding of ultimate things.

Research Project: Bibliography Search

NAME: _____ CLASS HOUR: _____ DATE: _____

Describe any experiences of serendipity in which you came across a book or section of a book by accident that really helped clarify a question in your mind. Also describe what questions you were seeking answers for, or what concepts you were trying to find explanations for. Did you have an experience of relief (catharsis) caused by finding good information?

Research Project: Bibliography Search

NAME: .... CLASS HOUR: .... DATE: ....

Describe how your research so far has been an experience of letting learning take its course. Among the things you've read, what are aspects seem to please you, and what seems to be stuff you must still grapple with, as it is desired by the nature of the human intellect to know truth?

Reflections on College-Level Research: Hits to One's Body of Understanding

NAME: _____ CLASS HOUR: _____ DATE: _____

This activity is likely causing cognitive dissonance, and yet that is part of the process that leads to liberation. That is the danger of putting your body of assumptions on the line for freedom. We can all be thankful that at least you aren't putting your physical body on the line. So you owe it to soldiers to dive deep into your experience of freedom. And this involves moving outside your present matrix of understanding, a matrix that is just a spotlight on reality.

As "mental warriors," you are to become a heroic reader. You know that what you read is threatening your present body of understanding. That body is taking hits–shrapnel, bullets to the torso–but how is it that we can resurrect that body of assumptions? Hint: What gets hit are the images triggered by key words you learned in grade school. You have detached that image from the word, and the image is being threatened. But you will have a more complex image linked to that word, an image that will come to mind when you see that word in the future.

How has your experience so far made you a "heroic reader"? What images are being examined and developed?

CHAPTER 10

Research Paper Mechanics

Goals:

- Know the general rules for citing and listing sources in MLA format.
- Know the general rules for citing books and journal articles in MLA format.

Outcomes:

- Edit drafts for proper citation mechanics.
- Write bibliographies correctly.

This chapter is pretty sedate, compared to the others chapters that are attempting to reshape or re-organize your intellect as you go through the period of transition from having an inadequate adult intellectual structure to one that is adequate—perhaps even enlightened.

This chapter is merely about the mechanics of citing sources in academic papers. But, there is wisdom in the saying that if you take care of the little things, the big things will take care of themselves.

Now, most students in college will not be staying in college after they earn a degree; most will return to the "civilian" life from whence they came. Most of them will not be staying in the academy, but while here, they are being asked to produce writing that adheres to the formal features that are preferred by the academic. Writing at the academic level isn't bad in itself, as long as the student understands its limits and virtues.

Also, since the academy does analyze all the institutions that the student will return to as a civilian after college, the civilian should know the best that has been thought about these institutions (especially its critique of these institutions and the adults in them).

You will be reading the results of careful exercises in critical thinking, and if you don't become an academic, you at least should be developing

1. your own top-flight critical thinking skills,
2. an enlightened perspective on the universe of human discourse, and
3. a set of specific skills for a job.

There arises, though, a two-headed issue for the student during college-level research: (1) understanding the language of scholarship and (2) using the citation conventions of the academy when presenting research findings, findings that are conveyed in wording that is accurate and precise. Students have to learn the preferences of the academic when it comes to writing structures and citing sources, even though once they leave college, they will be using civilian language preferences—and likely not citing sources at all.

So this chapter covers the citation mechanics that those following the MLA (Modern Language Association) format will need to know, and also features a shorter section on APA (American Psychological Association) format. In addition, the basics of citing journal articles and articles from popular magazines will be covered.

Overview: Citation Mechanics for a Research Paper

When you are tasked with writing a research paper, you will have to cite your sources in two major areas:

- within the essay, with what we call in-text citations, and
- in the bibliography.

You also need to be aware that there is a title given to the bibliographies listed at the end of the research paper:

- In MLA format, the list of bibliographies is called Works Cited.
- In APA format, the list is called References.

Bibliographies

One difference between this textbook and typical ones on college writing is that this book does not list all the bibliographical formats for all the different kinds of sources that could be used in a research paper. It's been my experience that these things can be easily found online.

But I would like to use this chapter to highlight what seems to be typical student questions about what to include in almost any bibliography and where to find that information. My information assumes that students are only using books from a library. I know that is a grave limitation, but it is also obvious that books are gravely underutilized by today's college student. Because the research project presented in this text requires that students only use books (journals are also applicable, but our time constraints rule them out, for now), I present information relevant to them.

One-author books: The format for a single-author book is probably the one students know (and even Web site formats try to follow this format as closely as possible). The bibliography begins with the author's last name, then first name, followed by the book title. Then comes the city of publication, the name of publisher, and the copyright year. NOTE: Book titles are either underlined or italicized.

Merton, Thomas. *Conjectures of a Guilty Bystander*. New York: Holt, 1966.

Book with two or three authors: List all the authors, but only the first author has the name reversed. The other names are listed first name first.

Merton, Thomas, James Fox, and Daniel Berg. *Conjectures of Bystanders*. Louisville: Trappist Press, 1988.

Note: Bibliographies begin flush left, and then any other lines needed are indented, as in the above example.

Book by an editor: The edited book is often an anthology, which the editor put together by selecting essays from a variety of different authors. The editor arranged the essays in a certain order and may have written an introduction. To cite the **anthology**, the first element is the editor's name, then the book title, city of publication, name of publisher, and copyright year.

Koch, Bill, ed. *The Ways of the World*. Dubuque: Holmstead, 2010.

A work from an edited work (an anthology): When you take one chapter or essay out of an anthology, you begin the entry with the name of the author of the essay, and you then give the name of the essay or chapter in the anthology, then the title of the anthology. The editor's name is placed after the book title.

Merton, Thomas. "The Bystander of Conjectures." *The Ways of the World*. Ed. Bill Koch. Dubuque: Holmstead, 2010.

Note: Chapter titles or article titles are NOT underlined or italicized. You put them in quotation marks.

Book with a translator: When you have a book written by a non-English writer that has been translated, you will need to cite the translator. But the bibliography begins with the writer's name.

Watson, Bill. *The World and Its Ways*. Trans. Fred Wynn. New Dubuque: House
Steady, 2002.

Two or more books by the same author: The first entry will give the author's name, with the rest of the bibliographical material, and then for the second and subsequent books, instead of writing the author name, you supply three dashes and a period. List the books alphabetically by book title.

Merton, Thomas. *The Seven Storey Mountain*. New York: Giroux, 1948.
___. *Zen and Zen Masters*. New York: Giroux, 1978.

Book other than first edition: You don't need to cite the edition of the book when it is the first edition. But for all editions after the first, mention the edition after the book title.

Watson, Bill. *The World and Its Ways*. 4th ed. Trans. Fred Wynn. New Dubuque: House
Steady, 2002.

The following is an important convention to apply to anthologies: When you have **two or more articles from an anthology**, you will need to make a bibliography for each article, as each article is by a different author. This means you will have to make at least three different bibliographies, but there will be no repetition of information. Here is what you will need:

First, a bibliography for the edited anthology itself:

Koch, Bill, ed. *Writers on the World's Way*. Dayton: Nighttime Press, 2006.

Second, you will need a bibliography for each of the articles (chapters) that you used from that anthology. BUT, each entry begins with the name of the author of that chapter, and then you include the chapter title in quotation marks. After the chapter title, you put only the last name of the editor and then the page numbers of that chapter. You DO NOT include the publisher information again.

Sisson, Edward. "Teaching the Laws in Darwinism." Koch 89–99.
Gudski, James. "Accept No Imitations: The Rivalries in Natural Law." Koch 100–125.

You would then list each entry alphabetically, by the first word of the bibliography (which is ordinarily—as in this case—the last name of the author or editor). For example:

Works Cited

A

B

C

....

Gudski, James. "Accept No Imitations: The Rivalries in Natural Law." Koch 100–125.

H

I

J

Koch, Bill, ed. *Writers on the World's Way*. Dayton: Nighttime Press, 2006.

L

M

N

....

Sisson, Edward. "Teaching the Laws in Darwinism." Koch 89–99.

T

U

V

....

To repeat, when citing TWO OR MORE works from an anthology,

- make an entry for each chapter author, and

- an entry for the anthology.

- REMEMBER: Only the anthology entry has all the bibliographical info.

Periodical Bibliographies

Although this course's research project does not require you to use journal articles, there will come a time when you will find journals useful in your research, and so I've included some information that will help to create the proper bibliographies for those journals.

There are several distinctions that you will need to make, the first being among the most important: determining the type of journal you are citing.

Determining the Kind of Periodical You Have:

- Be aware of the difference between popular magazines and scholarly journals.

- You will want to mostly use scholarly journals to carry the weight of your thesis.

- I will put a * by key distinctions to note in the following diagram.

HOW THE **LOOK** OF EACH KIND OF PERIDOICAL DIFFERS

POPULAR magazine:
Has ads, colorful.
No bibliographies
after articles
Pagination ALWAYS by issue

SCHOLARLY journal:
Has few ads, plain
Has bibliographies and/or
footnotes after articles
*Pagination:

Date:

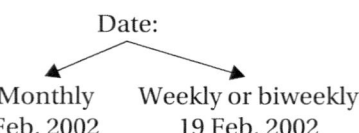

Monthly
Feb. 2002

Weekly or biweekly
19 Feb. 2002

By Volume:
need volume
number only:
54 (2002)

By Issue:
need volume
and issue:
54.2 (2002)

Here's how to write a bibliography for **popular magazines:**

Note: The distinction you must make is whether the magazine is **published weekly or monthly**.

For POPULAR magazines the bibliography entry ALWAYS needs the DATE. Example of WEEKLY popular periodical:

Lapham, Lewis. "Prairie Skies over Urban Smog." *Time* 12 Mar. 2005: 2–3.

If a popular magazine is a MONTHLY periodical, you just use (of course) the month.
Example:

Buchanan, Pat. "Republicans and Demos." *Harper's* Feb. 2005: 53.

Note: Months are abbreviated except May, June, and July.

Some names of popular magazines are: *Time, The New Republic, Harper's.*

Here's how to write a bibliography for **scholarly journals**:

Note: The distinction you must make is whether the journal is PAGINATED by issue or by volume.

If a journal is **paginated by volume**, the bibliography **doesn't need an issue number**—why? Because there is only one page 10 or page 50 in the volume.

This means that when you go to, say, the 1990 volume of Journal of Television, you will see that the late pages have high page numbers. That's because each issue's first page begins with the number where the last issue left off.

Example of bibliographical format for journal paginated by volume:

Ryan, Katy. "Revolutionary Schlock." *Journal of Television* 34 (1990): 451–55.

If a scholarly journal is **paginated by issue,** the bibliography **MUST include the issue number**—why? Because now you will find "page 10" 12 times in the volume. That is, each issue begins with page 1.

Example of bibliographical format for a journal paginated by issue:

Ryan Katy. "Schlock for the Scholar." Journal of Scholars 44:3 (2000): 44–66.

Some names of SCHOLARLY periodicals: *Journal of Popular Culture, American Quarterly.*

In-Text Citations: How to Cite Sources within the Essay

Basic Rules

Whether you summarize, paraphrase, or quote a source, you must cite sources. To repeat: Even when you summarize or paraphrase a source, you must cite the source of that information. That is, you must identify your author by name and give a page number (when the source is a paper product).

Two elements are required in a sentence that has information from your source:

- In EVERY PARAGRAPH, somewhere you need to cite the first word that begins a bibliography entry in the Works Cited list (most often an author's last name).
- The page number is needed, and is ALWAYS IN PARENTHESES.

The **author's name** can be located in several places:

1. In your writing, as part of a summary or paraphrase, as in this example:
   Allan Bloom suggests that rock's roots are in Plato's philosophy (24).
2. Or, in your writing, in connection with a quotation, as in this example:
   The professor of political philosophy, Allan Bloom, contends, "Rock music has its roots in Greek thought" (24).
3. THEN, the other major place you can put the first word of the bibliography (again, likely the author's last name) is in parentheses, as in this example:
   Rock music seemed to emerge from Plato (Bloom 24).
4. NOTE: If you mention the sources name in your sentence, you DON'T need to repeat the name in parentheses.
5. **It is good to mention the source name early in paragraphs, so as to avoid confusion.**

In all cases, the reader understands that the Works Cited page will contain—under the Bs—"Bloom" as the first word in the bibliography.

Punctuation concerns for sources cited within your paragraphs:

1. No matter how you present information from you source in a paragraph, when the sentence ends with a parenthetical citation, there is a period after the parenthetical cite, and NEVER before it.

   The period always goes after the parentheses, even with a direct quotation:

   a. "Rock music was born out of classical ashes" (Bloom 24).

   b. "Rock music," Bloom feels, "was born out of classical ashes" (24).

   c. The music of the 60s seems to be linked to classical music (Bloom 24).

   d. "Rock music was born out of classical ashes," observes Bloom (24).

   e. Music of today, what our kids like, seems to have been "born out of the ashes of classical music" (Bloom 24).

2. Question marks and exclamation points are retained within quotes, but still a period follows the parentheses:

   a. "Rock music was born out of classical ashes?" (Bloom 24).

   b. "Rock music was born out of classical ashes!" (Bloom 24).

Note on the use of commas within parentheses:

1. You do not put a comma between the author name and the page number when both are in parentheses.

2. However, when your Works Cited list has more than one work by a writer, you can cite the book title—in abbreviated form—in parentheses.

3. Then you do use a comma between the author's last name and the book title—but NO comma between book title and page number:

   a. The music of the 60s seems to be linked to classical music (Bloom, *Closing* 24).

4. Another option: You could mention the book title in your sentence:

   a. In his book *The Closing of the American Mind*, Allan Bloom claims that rock music has roots in classical music (24).

The use of *that* before a quote:

1. Sometimes it is logical to not use a tagline before a quote but let the grammar of the quote complete the grammar that you began in your sentence.

2. When that occurs, you will likely precede the quote with the word *that* and so construct this kind of sentence:
   a. Koch believes that Frye was correct when he wrote that "before too long, all adults will get a CLEW" (23).
3. Often, though, students use punctuation that is used with a tagline, and so they incorrectly write this:
   a. Koch believes that Frye was correct when he wrote that, "Before too long, all adults will get a CLEW" (23).
4. One way to check your work is to ask: If this entire sentence were my own writing—so there are now quotation marks—would I have put a comma after *that* and capitalized *before*?
5. ALSO NOTICE: Often there is a tagline verb just before *that*, as you see in the above example. So you could drop *that* and then preserve the comma and capitalized first word of the quote. See that?

The use of colon before a quote:

1. When you precede a quotation with several words and the words are an independent clause, use a colon instead of a comma:
   a. Frye's overall viewpoint expresses several key features: "The university functions to produce intellects that possess a universality of knowledge, combined with astute analytical skills and humane but tempered affections" (33).

Quotations have other unique concerns:

1. NEVER drop a quotation into the text without giving some kind of context to it. For example, don't do this:

   "Rock music is superior to Mozart" (Bloom 24). But when you think about it, Mozart's music is a lot different from rock and roll.

2. Always introduce a quotation with some kind of remark about it. For example:

   After studying music through the ages, Bloom concluded, "Rock music is superior to Mozart" (24).

3. Especially for a block quotation, always introduce it. Tell readers why they should read it, or what concept to look for. Here's an example:

   Allan Bloom suggests in the following remarks that music is much more than pretty sounds or can be used for more than just a distraction:

According to Plato, music is the barbarous expression of the soul. Barbarous, not animal. It arises out of the non-rational, inarticulate feelings of the soul. As such, it resists being tamed by words, which have their origins in reason. Furthermore, music arose in religious services, with a mixture of cruelty and awe. So music arises out of profound human need. (34)

More about block quotations:

- If your quotation is more than three lines long, block it as I did above. Note two differences in mechanics:
  - NO quotation marks are used (unless they are in the original material).
  - You place the period **before** the parentheses.

Another quotation concern: signal phrases (also called taglines)

- For your signal phrases, try to find a verb that fits the context of the quote.
- Don't use "Bloom writes" or "Bloom says" much if at all.
- Here are verbs that convey tone and action:
  - acknowledges, comments, endorses, reasons, adds, admits, concedes, denies,
  - emphasizes, suggests, observes, declares, claims

One tagline per quote:

- Use only one tagline per quotation.
- Avoid combining taglines, as in this example:

  Frye noted, "The adults in our modern society often never use an adult level understanding," he wrote, "and because of that, the crises of the economy continues" (55).

- Make sure such uses of taglines are not in your final drafts.

Variations with the Usage of Signal Phrases (Also Called Taglines)

Placement of Signal Phrases

Always introduce a quotation with a signal phrase, but vary the placement of that signal phrase.

Signal phrase before a quotation:

Allan Bloom admits, "When it comes down to it, I liked some of that early rock music, like ol' Bill Haley and the Comets" (22).

Signal phrase within a quotation:

"I liked to imagine, " admits Allan Bloom, " that some of that early rock music, like ol' Bill Haley and the Comets will live on forever" (22).

Note: Put the signal phrase early in a quote, after a few words. **Avoid putting the tagline between sentences that you are quoting.**

> NOT GOOD: "I like rock and roll because of the beat," notes Bloom. "It tends to lift my spirits" (44).
>
> THIS IS GOOD: "I like rock and roll," notes Bloom, "because of the beat. It tends to lift my spirits" (44).

Signal phrase after a quotation:

"I liked some of that early rock music, like ol' Bill Haley and the Comets," Allan Bloom admits (22).

In addition to those three basic signal phrase placements, try to use the following variations.

Signal phrase at beginning of sentence, mentioning the author's credentials:

Martha Bayles, who writes on cultural issues, explained, "For my title, I borrow[ed] the name from a song written by Johnny Green and most famously recorded by Coleman Hawkins in 1939" (59).

Signal phrase within a quotation, mentioning the author's credentials:

"For my title," the cultural critic Martha Bayles explained, "I borrowed the name from a song written by Johnny Green and most famously recorded by Coleman Hawkins in 1939" (59).

Signal phrase at the end of a quotation that mentions her credentials and deletes part of the quotation, using ellipses:

"For my title, I borrow the name from . . . Coleman Hawkins," wrote Martha Bayles, a critic of American culture (59).

When you paraphrase or summarize material from a source, you can mention the author's name in your writing:

Hacker suggests that you put the signal phrase in different places within the quotation and that you use different terms in referring to the source (582).

When you paraphrase or summarize material, you can put the author's name in parentheses:

Resist the urge to use a lot of long quotations linked together by a few of your own words because that style doesn't make for smooth writing (Hacker 582).

You will find that often you will structure the quotation so no comma is needed before the quotation:

Hacker suggests that you don't want to use a lot of quotations using "your own words only for connecting passages" (582).

Plagiarism

Plagiarism should become less of an issue if students have become so engaged with their words that they will want to discover for themselves how they can integrate ideas from texts they read into their structure of understanding (even if as a foe to their present assumptions about their values), and so they will want to read the words of others who have engaged deeply with their words.

But students are often unclear as to when they need to cite sources. And so, it is often the case that students plagiarize unintentionally. Here is the basic rule: **Even if you use your own words to convey an idea you get from a source, you need to cite the source by name and give the page number.**

Another snag I've encountered is that students will lift sentences directly from the text, and cite the source and page number, but they have not put quotation marks around the sentences that they took verbatim from the text. But this is plagiarism, because the reader will assume that the felicitous word choices and sentence structures are those of the student, and that would not be true.

But only 25 percent of the essay should be direct quotation (and not less than 15 percent), so the rest of the essay must be summaries or paraphrases of the source's information.

Summaries and Paraphrases

What's the **difference** between summaries and paraphrases?

- Summaries are shorter than the original.
- Paraphrases are as long as or longer than the original.

How are they **the same**?

- Both require you to use your own wording.
- Both require you to use your own sentence structures.

Your Sentence Structures have to be Different?!

Yes, that does sound disturbing, but remember that reader expectations illuminate the sentence structures, so you can come up with possible rewrites by remembering the following:

- If a sentence is in active voice, make it passive voice.
- If a sentence is in passive voice, make it active voice.

- Reverse the sequence of information.
- Change verbs into nominalizations.
- Change nominalizations, participles, gerunds, and infinitives into verb-verbs.

As you can see, there are many ways to create your own sentence structure. Practice paraphrasing— remember:

- Every sentence is rephrased.
- Every sentence can be longer than the original.
- You must use different sentence structures than the original.

ALSO: Expect your first attempts or first drafts of a paraphrase and summary to be rough and to need revision, either to bring out all the elements of a statement (as in a paraphrase) or to be more concise and have much fewer words, as in a summary.

APA Format

The sciences ordinarily follow the citation format of the American Psychological Association called APA style. This format highlights the year that a piece is published, because with the sciences, it is important to stay current with the latest research, just in case some long-held tenet is overthrown. (Such concerns are not as prominent in the humanities, where some insights into life seem to have already withstood the "test" of time.)

For in-text citations in APA style, keep the following in mind:

1. Usually just the last name is cited with even the first reference to a source.
2. Then the year of publication is placed right after the source's last name, in parentheses.
   a. **Example:** Benjamin (1982) offered an explanation based on a series of tests he ran in 1981.
3. When you have a quotation, the page number is often given and "p." is used in parentheses.
   a. **Example:** Benjamin (1982) concluded, "Adults can get through the period of transition if they detach their beliefs from their understanding of them" (p. 182).

For bibliographies:

1. The list of sources in APA format is called "References."
2. There are differences between APA and MLA.
   a. The year is placed right after the author name.

b. Only the first word of the title is capitalized, and any words that normally would be capitalized (e.g., proper nouns).

   c. The author first name is always abbreviated with initials.

3. **Example:** Benjamin, A. (1982). *Liberal Education is adult education.* New York: Bantam.

 # Correcting Bibliography Formats

NAME: .... CLASS HOUR: .... DATE: ....

Find errors in the following bibliographies and rewrite them in the spaces provided.

Annotated Bibliography

Hendel, Ronald. The Book of Genesis: a Biography. Princeton University Press, Princeton NJ.: 2013.

REWRITE: ....

Most of this book is about how Genesis has been interpreted over historical periods. The first chapter discusses three literary sources for Genius. These are based such consideration as grammar, style, and content. These authors can also be found throughout out the *Old Testament*. Detailed but entertaining to read.

Paul. Johnson, *darwin: Portrait of a genius*. New York – Penguin Group. 2012.

REWRITE: ....

Charles Darwin changed forever how we view the creation of the world and its development. When Darwin left on his voyage on the Beagle he believed in the Genius story of the creation of the world. He came to see that nature acted on individual orgasms to change species. Short book.

Johnson, Paul. *Intellectuals*. FIRST EDITION 1988. New York, Harper & Row.

REWRITE: ....

Johnson has a chapter on Karl Marx. He says Marx had more impact on events and ideas than anyone else in modern times. Marx ideas come from his poetic vision not from careful investigation or observation. Johnson argues that Marx was "incompetent in handling money."

Makari, George and Marquart, Lee. Editors *Revolution in Mind*: The Creation of Psychoanalysis. New York: Harper Collins Books, 2008.

REWRITE:

> This is more than a biography of Freud. It is a detail history of psychoanalysis. It argues the sources of Freud's ideas came from many authors such as Shakespeare, Nietzsche, and Pierre Janet among others. A long book that is filled with detailed discussion.

> Eissfeldt, Otto. Translator – Thurman, Carl _The Old Testament: An Introduction_. New York, Harper and Row Publishers: 1965.

REWRITE:

> This book discusses the pre-literary stages that went into the making of the Old Testament. This book is also translated in German throughout the text showing the relation to the Old Testament and the German descent. It is an interesting book but hard to read.

> Ernest Scott Findlay _The Literature of the New Testament_ New York, Columbia University Press: 1932.

REWRITE:

> The book discusses why these book are named "New Testament" and it goes into each book of the New Testament discussing its origin and how it relates to this idea of a "new" testament. This allows readers to see the person behind the book name and to also see how this person effected this religion and why his story was placed in this "new" section of the bible.

> Goodspeed, Edgar J. _The Story of the Bible_. Chicago: The University of Chicago Press, 1936.

REWRITE:

> This book discusses each book of the Bible and its purpose. The author discusses the meanings for these books and why they are placed into the Old or New Testament. This book all together gave me as the reader a glimpse as to what the Bible's purpose.

> Kendall. Booth. Henry. The Background of the Bible: a Handbook of Biblical Introduction. New York, Charles Scribner's Sons: 1928.

REWRITE:

> This book focuses not only on Old Testament theology but also on biblical theology and relates it as a branch or subheading of systematic theology. This book was more in depth than I was able to understand.

Correcting In-Text Citations

NAME: .... CLASS HOUR: .... DATE: ....

Identify and correct the citation errors in the following sentences.

Stephen Brookfield feels that adult thinking should be, "Attentive to the importance of context, and the validity of situational or relativistic reasoning," while remaining "committed to those values and general beliefs we find most valid for our experience." (15)

1. Describe the errors in this statement:

2. Rewrite the sentence with the citation mechanics corrected:

He also spoke of adults facing, "Discrepancies between uncritically assimilated norms governing moral conduct", (99) a state of affairs which I accept as a reality for a lot of adults.

3. Describe the errors in this statement:

4. Rewrite the sentence with the citation mechanics corrected:

Another cliché is conveyed when Brookfield writes that, "An increased ability to take alternative perspectives on familiar situations." (33).

5. Describe the errors in this statement:

6. Rewrite the sentence with the citation mechanics corrected:

Correcting Errors in Quotations

NAME: .... CLASS HOUR: .... DATE: ....

Correct the errors in the following quotations.

1. Starks states "A musician must repeat scales every day for years to get freedom of motion." (56)

REWRITE: ....

....

2. In the essay when she states "writing begins in childhood only the adult can do adult writing" (67) you can just tell from that sentence how important writing is to her.

REWRITE: ....

....

3. Holland observes that "Adults assume they don't need to examine their under-standing," there she gives the word understanding a very broad meaning, and also something completely different (Halland 66).

REWRITE: ....

....

4. Another thing that Bauman talks about is, "talent in writing is over rated" (Bauman 9).

REWRITE: ....

....

5. Another statement from Bauman that sticks out to me is, "writing is hard work" (p. 1).

REWRITE: ....

....

6. One new idea Bauman proposes is to, "write with a real purpose"(9).

REWRITE:

7. Another interesting claim Bauman has is that, "Talent in writing is overrated" (9).

REWRITE:

8. There are many things that Bauman states; another one being, "Most topics are not exciting" (16).

REWRITE:

9. "all mediocre writers share two qualities Bauman writes" (p. 2).

REWRITE:

10. "If they wished writes Bronson C. Keteler to leave out a part of a manuscript, they did it, (32)."

REWRITE:

Correcting Citation Mechanics

NAME: .... CLASS HOUR: .... DATE: ....

Change each citation so that the word *is* doesn't appear as part of the tagline, and correct any other citation errors.

Example:

Another thing that Bauman talks about is, "talent in writing is over rated" (Bauman 9).

Corrected: Besides describing how to start a writing project, Bauman also claimed, "Talent in writing is overrated" (8).

1. Another statement from Bauman that sticks out to me is, "writing is hard work" (p. 1). [Put the tagline at the end of the quote.]

Corrected: ....

....

2. Now, one thing that continues to appear on the pages in front of me is "talent in writing is overrated" (Bauman, 9). [Act like the entire statement is Bauman's and put the tagline inside the quote.]

Corrected: ....

....

3. One new idea Bauman proposes is to, "write with a real purpose"(9). [Put the tagline before the quote.]

Corrected: ....

....

4. The next bolded statement that Bauman said that was raised from the page was, "Almost all mediocre writers . . . ." (16). [your choice for placement of the tagline]

Corrected: ....

....

5. Another interesting claim Bauman has is that, "Talent in writing is overrated" (9).

Corrected:

6. The last important idea that I think Bauman says is, "Expose your feelings" (1).

Corrected:

7. There are many things that Bauman states; another one being, "Most topics are not exciting" (16).

Corrected:

8. Another Bauman statement I also decided to take to heart was, "Almost all mediocre writers share two qualities" (2). [Use a colon.]

Corrected:

9. What Bauman writes is, "all mediocre writers share two qualities" (2). [NOTE: what are the two ways of fixing this?]

Corrected:

Corrected:

CHAPTER 11

Our Historical Context and Our Historic Consciousness, Seen in the Light of Imaginative Literacy

The realistic turn of mind which marks our civilization and is probably a sign of our coming-of-age as a race, is further manifested in our rigorous standards of historical fact. This is not at all the same thing as scientific fact. (Langer, *Philosophy in a New Key* 228, 231)

To the historian, a miracle—though there were but one in the world—would be of great importance if it had consequences which ultimately involved many people. If there were any indubitable record of it which clearly established it as a miracle, history would simply accept it. (Langer 231)

This is a transformation of the mind, not of the body. By the standards of evolution, it will be cataclysmic, instantaneous. It has already begun. (Clarke, *Childhood's End* 184)

In this textbook on college-level writing (and reading), I've been arguing that college-level writing should be considered adult-level writing, and such writing is different from academic writing, though is the kind of writing that students largely read in college. But I also feel that not many academics are really thinking at the adult level. Certainly they have become more skillful with their critical thinking tools, but something more is yet required. I'm not making any moral judgments by saying this, either. Because I've gotten closer to attaining the historical consciousness that college represents, I can understand that in key ways, the lack of adult thinking is a developmental reality. But now, perhaps, due to this historical perspective, adults in college can now suggest why an intellectual perspective about and engagement with the intellect is now to be acquired by all adults. It's not so much that adults of our era have to be of goodwill, either—it's more that the human intellect is just growing or differentiating to this intellectual structure.

I've been involved with liberal education at some level since I entered college in the Fall of 1970, and one of the things I've concluded from my diverse encounters with the disciplines of liberal education (and this occurred to me, I think, around 40 years ago) is this: **Humanity is biology's self-conscious element.** We are **biology's second structure of consciousness,** aware of time as well as space. Instinctual animals are biology's first matrix of consciousness, only aware of spatial dimensions, although they also have sense organs and a brain, like humans do. They also make sounds, as humans do, but only humans have shaped sounds into words and then produced a written form of these words.

Instinctual animals arose hundreds of millions of years ago, if we have interpreted the fossil record correctly. Mammals arose 150 million years ago. The fossil record suggests that humans arose 2 million years ago, and our particular subspecies around 160,000 years ago.

Whether this is true or not, **a basic and unique phenomenon of the human animal is that it has the power of the word**, spoken or written.

But we should note that the written word did not exist until 6,000 years ago, and it appeared at the same time as trade and cities arose. And the first written language systems did not have the alphabet, which was invented just 3,000 years ago, and then adults inserted those markings into their existing writing systems that they'd been taught in childhood. And it is worth noting that most of the human achievements that we study in college arose after the alphabet was inserted into the language systems that had existed before then.

Now, in 2013, on American college campuses, students are utilizing their verbal language in a variety of ways, to learn more about art and science, business and culture, and they are doing this in a troubling economic and political environment.

But, it might be the case that they are not engaging with their words at the adult level, which I think is the college level (and to be distinguished from the "academic" level), and which is enlightened adult engagement with words, not an inadequate adult engagement with words.

If it is true that humanity is biology's second matrix of consciousness, I think **we can then speculate as to the likelihood of a third level of biological consciousness appearing, and what that level of consciousness might look like.** Based on the intellectual experiences generated by the activities in this book, I would suggest that this next level can aptly be called a "perfected consciousness" (as Chardin words it in the passage in the Epigrams). That term suggests that the adult knows that he or she isn't perfect, but knows the intellect has a process that is perfect (see the chapter on the writing process). I would also posit that you have tested this third level as a pattern of organization, or as a new organization of reality, as you moved throughout this book, and now see it as very useful (to say the least!).

So, it turns out that as you develop these rigorous protocols of critical thinking (steps of which have you explore the images triggered by words and have you use metaphors deliberately), and as you construct these speculations, you are building the third structure or level of biological consciousness.

Not that it's much to brag about. As Northrop Frye noted in his lectures gathered into *The Modern Century*, "It has frequently been remarked that we may be, if we survive, the primitives of an unknown culture, the cave men of a new mental era" (96).

And his wording leads me to ask two questions key to perceiving accurately our historical situation: (1) who is this "we" that is surviving and being "primitive" and reading these words; and (2) what is this thing called words that the "we" is receiving through listening and reading, and conveying through speech or writing?

As for the first question, following is a diagram of the two parts of one's self-image. It should be studied in conjunction with the diagram on the back inside cover that tries to organize the two basic parts of the human person. This chart organizes the basic parts of the human personality.

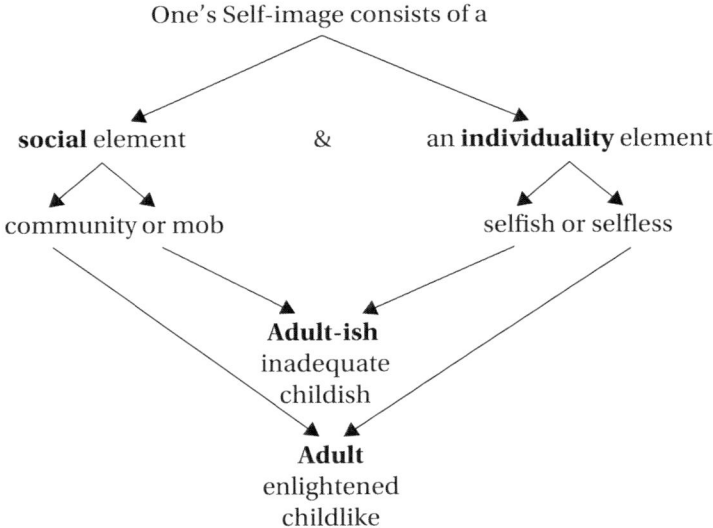

This diagram posits that the person is composed of contrasting elements, the social element and the individual element. Because each of us is (up until recently) the product of the union of two people, such a union implies a social environment out of which we arise. And then, during our childhood, we learn the basic social narratives of our society, the national and religious narratives. But there is a seat of consciousness in each of us, a sense of individuality, and this sense of individuality is prized by the democratic ethos. But as we get older, we are faced with a choice (and college asks students to face up to this choice). You can remain in the level of understanding that you bring into college, a level that is necessarily at the childhood level, and in keeping it, obtain just an inadequate adult understanding that leads to a mob mentality and a selfish relationship to the environment, or you can examine the body of understanding that you bring into college (or into the early adult years) and sacrifice those things that you had prized but that now seem to only perpetuate selfishness and a mob mentality. You see how the narratives of society can reflect a key part of any human consciousness (a sense of the universe of life residing in oneself), and you see that the true self arises through self-sacrifice.

And I would assert that we, as humans, clarify all of these features in ourselves as we seize control of the human mind's automatic use of metaphors, and we become skillful with a—if not THE—key tool that the mind uses to clarify its understanding of its environment: words.

In fact, we will even clarify our perceptions of ourselves, and we will have a more intense experience of that which is uniquely human: the human intellect. In seeing how our deliberate use of metaphor illuminates our perception (and use) of the human intellect, we explore a realm that right now seems to be the domain of a privileged few, but we (the few) will be finding ways to get others to break through into this universal human environment. In the words of the recent Vonage ad, these privileged few will be "crazy generous"!

Some Metaphors and Movies to Help Individuals Examine Their Lot in Liberal Education

1. Ever since commercial civilization arose 6,000 years ago, we humans in education have been having an agrarian revolution of the mind, plowing the mental fields of life's self-conscious element and growing new conceptions of human understanding with the written word.

2. The alphabet was introduced into existing language systems 3,000 years ago, and that was like the Industrial Revolution for the mind.

3. We in liberal education (LE) in 2013 have lost touch with the original power of the alphabet, and it is like we are stuck in the rigid old language systems that existed before the Phoenicians gave the alphabet to other literate people.

4. We need to sharpen the blades of our intellectual tools, which means using our words more deliberately.

5. When we become conscious of the powers of word, it is like we have begun the digital revolution for the mind.

6. It isn't that we make new things—instead it is as if all things now seem new.

7. We have scrubbed ideas off the structure of understanding that we brought into college that, had they remained, would make our adult thinking experiences frustrating.

8. But as Mark Van Doren writes in his book *Liberal Education*, "Good thought, like courage, is contagious."

9. Too many of us are like Prince Henry in the movie *Ever After*—he tried to escape his life of privilege because of the duties thrust upon him. If we in LE and commercial civilization *do not* face our duties of liberation (in the sense of detachment, not freedom of choice), we are evading our duties. We must produce historic mental crops and share them with others through our technology.

10. Not all people are in the structures of commercial civilization, so these insights into words are for those with a literacy heritage, but then because words are so basic to the consolidation of human consciousness, our insights are really the birthright of the human species.

11. We are then like Neo in *The Matrix* trilogy, sensing something is seriously wrong with the social environment we are in, but not knowing what to do. Liberal education is like Morpheus, and offers the student a way to see the "matrix."

12. For students in college writing and research courses, this means seeing the word–image dynamic and the structure that strings of words are expected to have (beyond grammatical correctness).

13. As students engage more deeply with the words they brought into college, they will be like Neo when he finally wakes up in that tub of goo—what I call an adult bassinet. He is physically fully grown (as most students are when they enter college), but he has been unconscious of how his nervous energy has been powering the Matrix. This is like students not knowing that their minds automatically use metaphors to convey facts.

14. When students submit to the disciplines of alphabet literacy, they will be like Neo at the end of *The Matrix*, when he could see the structure of the Matrix behind the specific images of the buildings and the virus-men.

15. Such outcomes could be evidence that life is showing its self-conscious element within LE the main threads that students can combine into the outline of Biological Consciousness Number Three (BC 3).

16. We see that words are the mightiest swords and when we examine the word-image dynamic that is going on in our mind, we organize our understanding of words (and ourselves) in liberating and refreshing ways from inadequate adult understanding.

17. With our swords of words, we put our bodies of assumptions in the line of critical fire, and are grateful that we are not putting our physical bodies in the line of actual bullets.

18. Our imagination compels us to construct (and live out) the narrative (about arriving at the adult understanding of narratives), and this intellectual work makes us be the change that we want to see in the world of commercial civilization.

I've provided you with a numbered list of ideas that have occurred to me over the past few years, and along with these ideas I've also come up with a device called wedges, which illustrate the basic distinctions that I believe root us in "imaginative realism," a term I came up with in 2009 after watching those chaotic congressional town hall meetings. While watching these citizens get irate over what they perceived to be a socialist takeover of medicine, I noticed that many who spoke this way had been young during the hottest times of the Cold War, which somewhat officially ended in 1989, and which by then had existed for some 40 years.

But words like "socialism" that were bandied about in 2009 were triggering images in the minds of these citizens of events that were likely to be 50 years old. And when students come into college, the words that they hear and read will be triggering images in their minds. One of the key activities I've explained in the book is that a key part of critical thinking is examining these images and identifying their history, strengths and weaknesses, and other aspects.

Of course, our national health care debate has been focused mostly on maintaining physical health, and I have no quarrel with that focus. But it does beg the question about the needs of psychological or mental health. I would submit that LE is all about giving students this mental health (through historical perspectives, which Northrop Frye felt was college's main duty), but we find out that mental health improves as we gain control of unconscious habits of thinking and expression as they relate to words, whether spoken or written, heard or read. As we improve our understanding of and engagement with the phenomena of words, we find that this intellectual work has improved our mental – and emotional – health in powerful ways.

We understand the word–image dynamic and understand how those images can affect the quality of adult thinking. We can deliberately use metaphors because we know that metaphors trigger in our mind images that the images triggered in our minds by metaphors help us to explore not just the issue being discussed but our understanding of and relationship to that issue. In engaging deliberately with this word-image phenomenon, we are making our thinking visceral as well as cerebral, and so our verbal expressions "pack a punch."

We also find out that until the adult undertakes this deeper engagement with words, he or she is likely in the grips of an imaginary realism that triggers real-enough anxieties. And sometimes those anxieties cause very real actions—regrettable actions. But as adults see this word–image dynamic and grow in wisdom about it, then they can recognize the imaginary in their sense of realism, and no longer are spooked by these imaginary realities. They then experience a psychosomatic catharsis that eventually has truly positive physiological consequences.

When we understand this health care distinction, we will then understand this one:

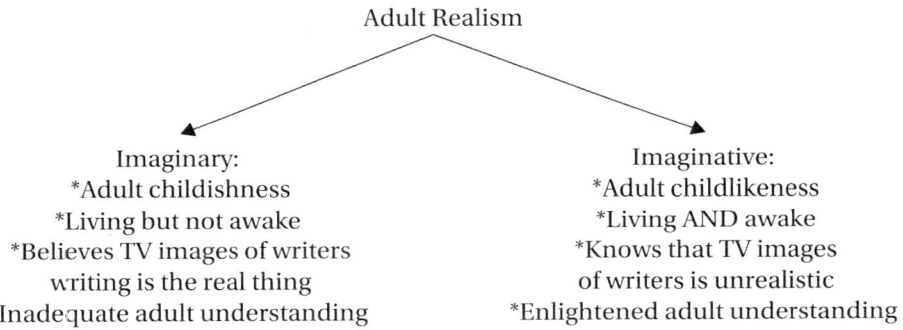

Adult Realism

Imaginary:
*Adult childishness
*Living but not awake
*Believes TV images of writers
writing is the real thing
*Inadequate adult understanding

Imaginative:
*Adult childlikeness
*Living AND awake
*Knows that TV images
of writers is unrealistic
*Enlightened adult understanding

You will notice that to be childlike, individuals must be adults, and individuals will be adults only by having a fully functioning imagination (and when the imagination knows that its early attempts at expression can be tentative and weak, a person knows that he or she is childlike). I would submit that the imagination will show us that the history of commercial civilization comes to a close when we apply our literary understanding to that history—its past, present and future

The gist of my explanations is that college education is not merely about acquiring skills for a job one gets after graduating from college. In very real ways, college education is adult education, and this means that adult education is radical and revolutionary, terms we apply to college. But if Mark Van Doren is correct in saying that there are essentially two stages to education—elementary and college—then we can say that there are two levels of understanding (childhood and adulthood), and we can even speculate that there are two periods of growing up, one in childhood and one in adulthood. But with the adult period of growing up, there is a period of transition involved before reaching this adult-level understanding (and there are two tiers of adult understanding). This first tier of adult understanding isn't achieved just by adding more information to the knowledge brought into college. There is something more fundamental that takes place, and it involves (1) understanding how understanding occurs,

(2) knowing how knowledge is produced, and (3) engaging more deeply with the phenomena of words. To quote Mark Van Doren, "Intellectual activity... is the search for truth, and truth found anywhere will have its affinities in other fields. A truth possessed is itself a kind of training, since it teaches us how to recognize reality" (LE 121).

When students achieve an adult-level engagement with words, and the narratives conveyed to them in childhood (via the use of words), then they can see that the entire structure of liberal education is really a diagram of the ecology of the human mind. The human mind has always had this structure, but it has only become clear to adults in the past 2,200 years, and only to adults in commercial civilization, and even within that population, only small numbers have (to date) really perceived well the elements of this ecology of the mind. Following are two schematics of this ecology of the mind. In both diagrams, replace "Liberal Education" with "Ecology of the Adult Mind."

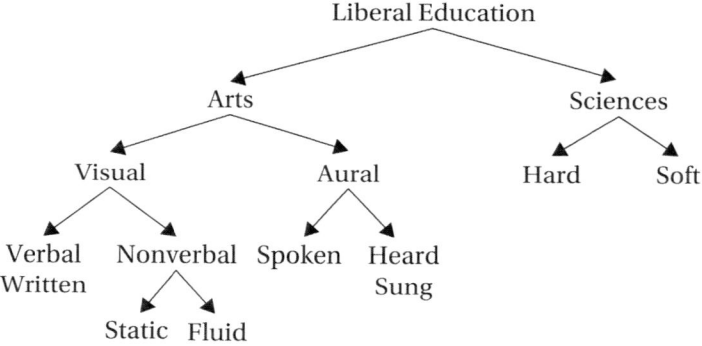

Based on my involvement with liberal education in some fashion over the past 40 years, I would like to offer this revamping of the basic elements of liberal education, and these elements seem to articulate more fully the basics of the adult human intellect (and again, you can replace "Liberal Education" with "Ecology of the Adult Mind"):

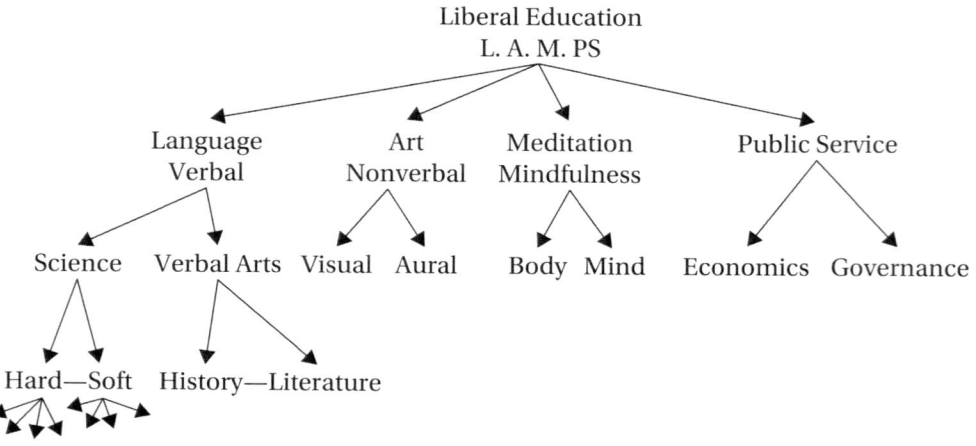

Based on the intellectual engagements I've been privileged to participate in, I'd also like to offer an outline of the basics of the human consciousness, biology's second structure of consciousness. Again, these elements have always existed in humanity, but we can say that we can now see these features with something like definitive clarity because of the uniqueness of commercial civilization – and its problems.

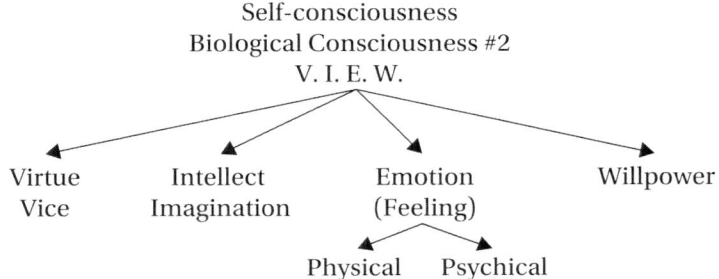

Self-consciousness
Biological Consciousness #2
V. I. E. W.

Virtue · Intellect · Emotion · Willpower
Vice · Imagination · (Feeling)

Physical · Psychical

A noteworthy feature of this diagram involves the linkage of elements that adults have assumed are mutually exclusive but which are really differing sides of the same phenomena.

Perhaps the most troubling is the virtue–vice tandem. It suggests that some virtues might really be vices. Students with a CLEW can see this, and how the virtuous are making moral judgments based on imaginary realism. This realism triggers real anxieties that then prompt actions that we eventually call vices, or immoral – at least regrettable. But adults with a CLEW have an imaginative realism, and this realism also triggers real anxieties, but at least they are based on a realism that sees things in an unbiased – objective – way. Eventually, imaginative virtues dissolve imaginary anxieties and vices disappear.

When adults achieve this level of adult thinking and understanding, they are then, again to use Mark Van Doren's words, developing the "intellectual virtues [that] free the person in understanding and discourse. The freedom of the intellect gives us possession of our last and greatest powers, the powers most characteristic of us as men. That these powers had been unsuspected renders their possession all the more miraculous" (122).

If I've articulated a very realistic outline of our historical situation, and have done so within the environment of liberal education, then there is one more step to outline, and that is the place of this intellectual work within our biological context. The following is a wedge that outlines our past, present, and future:

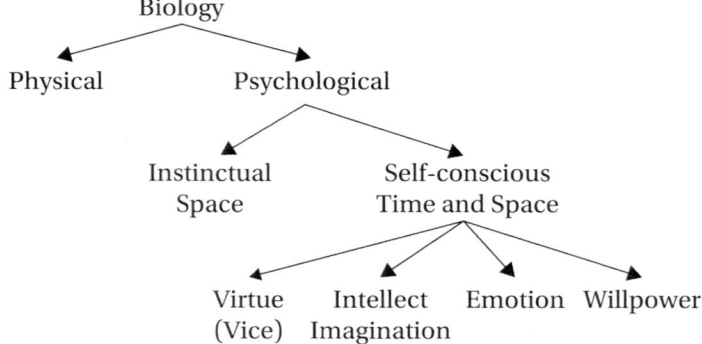

Were this wedge to suggest the length of time each element has existed, we'd have the word "Physical" in very big letters, the physical being around 15 billion years old, and Earth being around 4.5 billion years old. The psychical dimension of life—which Chardin says has only recently gotten life's attention—began in very primitive form some 500 million years ago, so it would be spelled with smaller letters than with what we spelled "Physical." The human species, being no more than 2 million years old, would be spelled even smaller, and then our latest social arrangement, commercial civilization, being only 6,000 years old, would have lettering the size of—oh—a flea!

Let me express this historical perspective with what I call the "3-Part Chart," two parts of which I used in the chapter on assumptions when discussing the two stages of education in the United States. As you might recall, Mark Van Doren said that education is composed of two parts – elementary and college. But as you know, students often go to college to help themselves attain a job after graduation, so in that way college helps them through the third part of this 3-Part Chart. Here is my illustration of the basic 3-Part Chart:

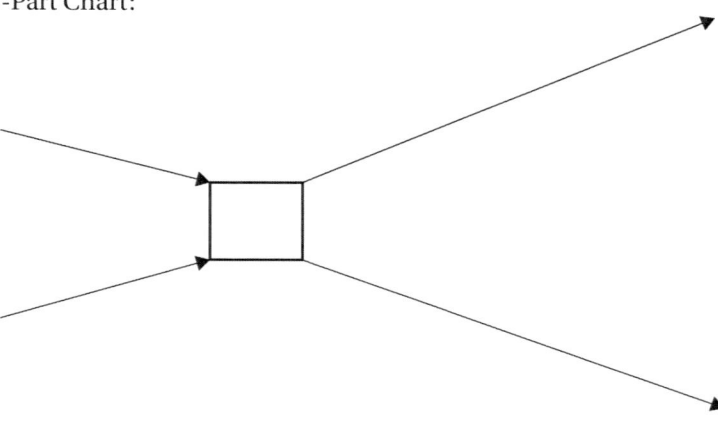

Here is the 3-Part Chart for education in the United States:

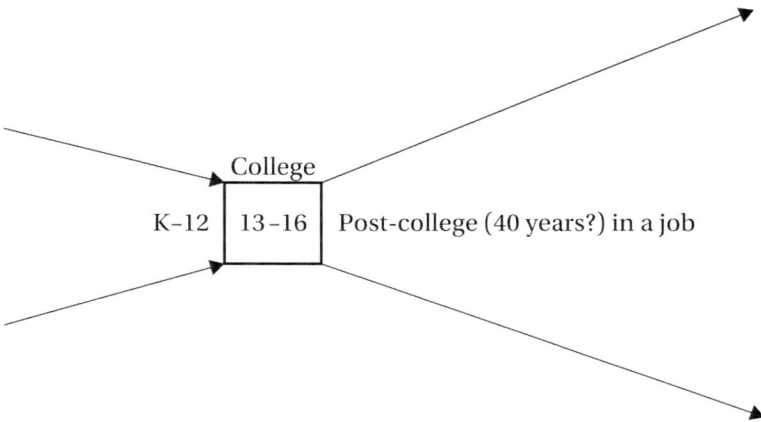

Notice that college is the shorter of the two educational periods, being only 4 years long (technically), and that K–12 is 13 years long; so, the first part is longer than the middle. But then after college, the student spends 40 years or so in a job before retirement, so the longest part is the third part. We can use this pattern to map out other phenomena important to the human species, although in most cases, the third element isn't as clearly perceived as it is in the education chart.

For instance, there have been two basic types of biological phenomena so far, the physical and the psychical, and they can be mapped out like this using the 3-Part Chart:

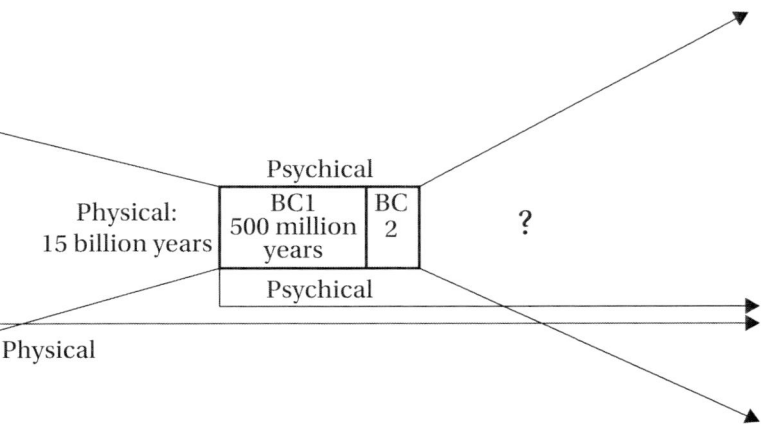

Historically, there have been two kinds or levels of consciousness so far, and their proportions reflect the proportions between the two stages of education for the adult in U.S. commercial civilization:

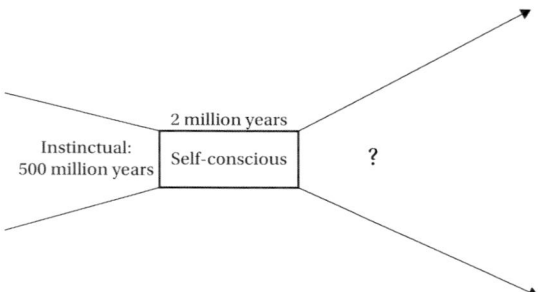

We can also organize the history of words into a 3-Part Chart:

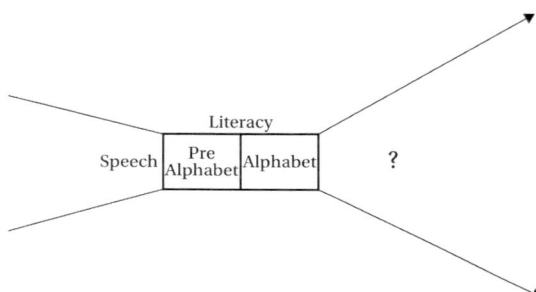

It should also be noted human society has had four social arrangements (hunter-gatherer, pastoral, agrarian, and urban), but we must note that the written word only arose with the last of these social arrangements, the urban. In comparison to hunter-gatherer life, urban life is very young.

We should also note that literacy underwent a radical transformation 3,000 years ago, and in some ways, we can associate this transformation with what the student should experience during the period of transition that occurs in college, during the general education portion of college education.

With that in mind, I'd like to offer detailed diagrams of the major intellectual activities that students in college can (should?) go through. First is the following:

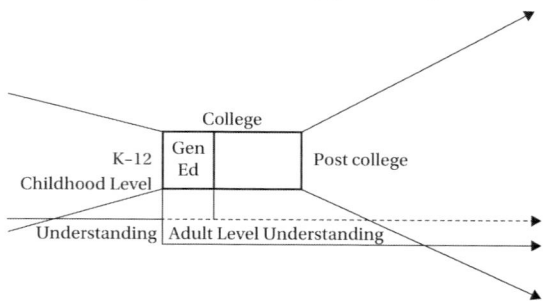

In this diagram, we see that the level of understanding that the student brought into college is necessarily the elementary level, and, for a period of time, this level of understanding is rubbing up against the college level of understanding. A mental fight occurs. Of course, students could choose to avoid this fight, and leave college with an inadequate adult understanding. Here is the second chart:

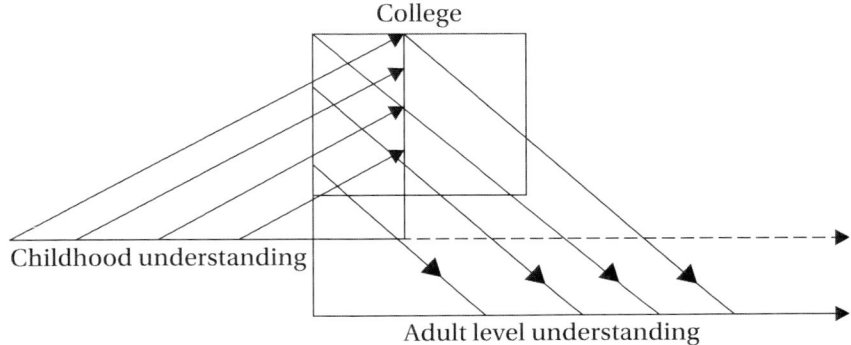

This chart illustrates the tension in students who retain the understanding they brought into college even though they face facts that challenge that understanding. They assume that their beliefs are being challenged, but if college can explain that it is only asking them to examine their understanding of those beliefs, students then become willing partners in the battle for clarification of understanding. This is represented as follows:

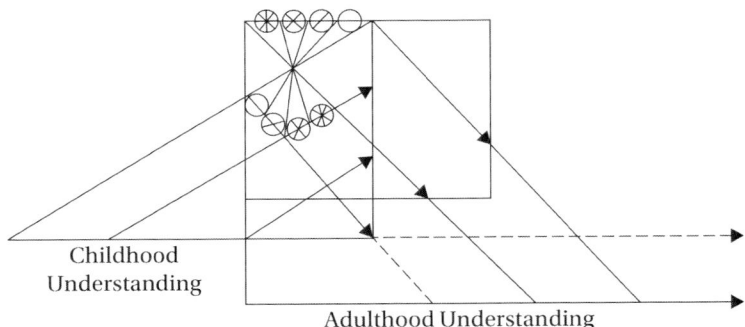

As part of this transition, students are asked to perceive how words trigger images in their minds. Those images (1) are likely simplistic, and (2) affect the quality of their thinking. If they can make the images more complex, they will engage more deeply with their words and so improve their chances of describing their understanding in wording that is more accurate and precise than it had been.

Students can then know that the period of transition is over, that they have adequate adult understanding, perhaps even an enlightened adult understanding. Certainly, they will know that they scrubbed some ideas off the structure of understanding that they'd brought into college—ideas that, had they remained, would have kept them in the darkness of an inadequate adult understanding. Students know now that those ideas are permanently removed. They might still have other questions and still can't influence the larger world of commercial civilization. But within each student's own "world," things are in relatively good and peaceful order. And students can articulate their explanations of things with wording that is more accurate and precise than it had been.

Here is how I tentatively describe our mythic phenomena:

1. Our economic problems can be seen as occurring because the natural expansion impulse of capitalism has reached its frontier closing point.

2. It is like the past 6,000 years of commerce have been the pioneer stage of economics for commercial civilization.

3. The closing of the economic frontier has caused a chaos of intellectual thought (what should we do?) and anxiety (will we ever get our economy revived?).

4. In addition, the cycle of culture has periods of exhaustion; adults in 2013 might be witnessing such a period of exhaustion, and they must find ways to revitalize the intellectual machinery.

5. We see that today's economic structure is of a piece with what began 6,000 years ago in the cradle of civilization, present-day Iraq.

6. That was the eastern side of the fertile crescent, the western side of which was the land of the Bible, of alphabet literacy.

7. The alphabet was introduced into existing language structures 3,000 years ago, structures that had existed for 3,000 years and had entered a period of exhaustion.

8. This alphabet brought flexibility and stability to an intellectual environment that in many ways is like ours, materially wealthy but also socially chaotic.

9. Those social structures of law and commerce and science that began then in isolated pockets of commercial civilization are now global, and they function like the digestive, respiratory, and circulatory systems of a social body.

10. The larger brain for this body is being developed in LE, and students of the twenty-first century can see their own minds as being a microcosm of this social brain.

11. We can say that this brain has just ended its infancy stage by the fact that American soldiers have been in the Middle East, the cradle of commercial civilization, risking their physical lives for freedom.

12. Students in LE will now risk their psychical lives for freedom, and this risky venture will justify the sacrifices—psychical and physical—that the soldiers have made.

13. The students will awaken their imagination within science, art, business, and education, and then see how their newfound organized structure of understanding—which we might want to call the Total Imaginative Form (TIF)—can eventually be "hammered" into the social institutions of commercial civilization.

14. One of the key virtues that LE can produce in students is being responsible with their words. And when students submit to the disciplines in this course, they learn to be responsible with their words.

15. Even more, they see how their intellectual engagement with their words is cogently represented by the image of the burning bush in the story of Exodus, and by the image of the lighted torch favored by the Greeks. In other words, their deeper engagement with and more objective view of words has lit a self-sustaining inner light and strength.

16. And students then are curious to engage with the words in other disciplines to see if those words will enlighten them, too—or if they can bring some light to those disciplines.

After students have gone through the disciplines of liberal education, they will have a sense of self that is different from the sense of self they brought into college. Having submitted to intellectual disciplines of LE, they will have scrubbed off those ideas that would likely have led them to practicing the worst behaviors of a mob-minded, egostistic self, and they will likely be heading toward a maturation of the adult-level self, having a mature sense of community (which entails a mature relationship with the universe of discourse) and a selflessness that is very satisfying. With the historical perspective proper to adult understanding, they will be aware that some very unfortunate social dynamics might still have to play out around them, but they are less prone to assume that such realities are the ultimate human realities. Instead, they will see not only the realities of crisis but of regeneration. Indeed, with their intellects, they are planting the verbal seeds of regeneration in the intellectual soils of those around them.

> We cannot by taking thought add a cubit to our statures;
> it is a change of worlds that is necessary,
> the lifting of the whole body
> to a fully imaginative plane
> by getting rid
> of the natural man.
>
> (Frye, *Fearful Symmetry* 194)

Perhaps the kinship between the primitive and ourselves goes even deeper: It has been remarked that we may be, if we survive, the primitives of an unknown culture, the cave men of a new mental era.

> (Frye, *The Modern Century* 96)

CHAPTER 12

Proto-Essays

> No genuine idea can be expressed in undeveloped speech or writing. . . . We have much less to fear from science than from a misuse of words. However uninhibited, it is not free speech, [but] free speech is the one aspect of a genuine society that we all hold in our hands, or mouths. *(Frye, The Well-Tempered Critic, p. 47)*

This chapter consists of essays that I have begun and that touch on aspects of life that liberal education examines, although the college student might be able to avoid facing these issues. But if you have put a good-faith effort into understanding the deeper engagement with words that I've tried to present in this textbook, you will likely be interested in the ideas presented in these "proto" essays.

A "prototype" is an original form of something, a first full-scale model to be replicated. The only things to be replicated here are an interest in the topic and a college level engagement with words.

Only several paragraphs of each essay are given, and after you read them, you will be asked a series of questions. You will be invited to complete each essay as you see fit, although you will need to explain why you chose the content you selected, and your word choices, using the vocabulary of PRE. The goal is to give you practice in using these various verbal tools in larger structures. And I want to suggest that in doing these activities, you are preparing to exercise the "one aspect of genuine society" that students hold in their metaphorical hands and mouths – and not so metaphorical hands and mouths.

I would also allude to something Mark Van Doren wrote, that in college, students begin their "study of the rules by which one may become a citizen in the republic of human understanding." Even more startling, he notes that we view "all men in their attempt to be the same man."

First Proto-Essay

A Compelling Conundrum for College: Openness to Alternative Perspectives versus Critical Thinking

As I've been developing my CWR course, I've been reflecting on how this course fits in with the LAC program and the mission of the University to provide students with "transformative learning experiences." In addition, the university seeks to provide an environment where everyone is treated with respect and everyone can feel "comfortable." As part of this process, students are asked to open their minds to "alternative perspectives," and to "think outside the box."

While all of this is good, sometimes in practice, the situation becomes mucked up because college is also supposed to teach "critical thinking skills," and involved with critical thinking is the making of judgments, and sometimes judgments of a controversial kind, involving the inadmissibility of some forms of evidence, some viewpoints or assumptions. But the popular conception of "openness" would seem to be in conflict with natural parts of critical thinking.

Then there is this—too often, students who are being open to alternative viewpoints are listening to the presentation (either with their ears or with their eyes) through a filter of presuppositions and prior experiences that makes their reception of these alternative viewpoints less than unbiased, although they seem attentive to what they are hearing (or reading). They filter what they are hearing (whether with their ears or with their eyes) through their minds, and their minds could be what I call a biased receptivity structure. I also venture to suggest that the person conveying this alternative viewpoint also possesses a "biased receptivity structure" (BRS).

And I think that the LAC program as a whole—or maybe it is just the writing course or the courses that focus on words—can help the students scrub those ideas off their structure of receptivity—their intellect—so it has an unbiased receptivity, an unbiased receptivity that improves their chances of making some quality critical judgments.

....

....

Causes of Persecution

At Mass today we sang "Blest are They," and the last verse sings, "Blessed are they who suffer hate, all because of me … rejoice and be glad, yours is the kingdom, shine for all to see." Depending on your experiences, those words will trigger in your mind images of persecutions that Christians have had since the time of Nero, and adults and children would be killed for professing their faith and resisting idolatry.

While such acts of self-sacrifice are laudable, I would ask that adults in our day be a bit more cautious in assuming that such acts of self-denial are needed or as meritorious as we've assumed.

I offer this kind of observation because today we can see more clearly the intellectual problems that have been the basis of some of these conflicts and so bring about what the Christian witness was intended to produce, but without the bloodshed (not the physical bloodshed). It is my observation that such conversations or confrontations are sterile and even counterproductive because both sides are not imaginative: both sides consist of adults who have inadequate adult understanding of the basics of human life. And basic among the basics is the phenomena of words and the experience of education.

....

....

Adult Resistance to Learning and Adults Learning about Resistance

In his book *Dealing with Resistance in Learning*, Stephen Brookfield writes, "Why people resist learning is a puzzling complex question, particularly when such resistance appears to come out of nowhere." I would have to respond with, "Not really. It is easy to understand why people can be resistant to learning."

It's been my impression that most students—and perhaps many college faculty—assume that learning is just a matter of consuming information. The student takes these tasty—or boring—morsels of knowledge and ingests them and they don't believe that the information will do much to change their body of understanding. But something happens when the "people" are faced with information about what we might call structural issues, issues related to what scholars call epistemology and hermeneutics. When we get information that asks us to examine what we believe counts as "knowledge," and that asks us to examine how we go about understanding something, it is that learning that affects the beliefs of a person as much as the intellect, and so the emotions of the adult are also agitated.

Of course, college education is all about having students—who usually are in their early adult years—examine the things that they had been taught in childhood and which they'd been told they would need to use during their adult years. When college asks students to examine what they were told were concepts and ideas—beliefs and narratives—that concerned the ultimate reality of things, it is then that the students will most likely be resistant (or bored, if the student is already fed up with mainstream ideas about ultimate or foundational realities).

But as I've told students—and I think this idea gets traction in their mind—they are being asked not so much to question the beliefs that they were taught in childhood as they are asked to question their understanding of these beliefs which deal with purported ultimate things. It is my thesis that they must get a radically different understanding of those things if they are to get an adult level understanding of those things. College seems to be where we get that adult level understanding, or begin the process of converting childhood understanding of ultimate things into adulthood level understanding of ultimate things (and hope the adult level understanding is closer to an ultimate understanding of ultimate things than the childhood level understanding is).

The adult who is resisting the knowledge that the college teacher is asking him or her to examine might not be making this distinction between a belief and one's understanding of that belief. Making a distinction between adult level understanding and childhood level understanding might also help the adult not be so uptight when considering the data that seems to impact their allegiance to a belief. If college (faculty) can set the conditions for learning such that the adult doesn't feel a flanking operation is being done on their most cherished beliefs, the student might be willing to take up the challenge of considering that the understanding of things they bring into college isn't at the adult level. I think there are several ways that the faculty can create use conditions.

....

....

Proto-Essay Analysis: Conundrums

Answer the following questions concerning the proto-essay on page 256, "A Compelling Conundrum for College: Openness to Alternative Perspectives versus Critical Thinking."

1. Which words in the title trigger images in your mind? Describe the images.

2. What seem to be the key terms in these paragraphs?

3. What seem to be the key concepts in these paragraphs?

4. What kind of opening does the proto-essay have?

5. What would you want to see in the very next paragraph?

6. What would you expect to read in the rest of the essay?

7. In what ways does this topic reflect your experience of college so far?

Proto-Essay Analysis: Persecution

Answer the following questions concerning the proto-essay on page 257, "Causes of Persecution."

1. What seem to be the key terms in these paragraphs?

2. What seem to be the key concepts in these paragraphs?

3. What kind of opening does the proto-essay have?

4. This section ends by announcing some examples. Based on what you've learned (if not come to believe) in this course, write the next paragraphs that seem to generate expectations of examples.

5. The title is a bit anemic. After you write the new material, come up with two or three possible titles.

6. In what ways does this topic reflect your experience of college so far?

Proto-Essay Analysis: Resistance

Answer the following questions concerning the proto-essay on page 257, "Adult Resistance to Learning."

1. Could I drop the word *with* just before I give my response to the quoted Brookfield statement? What would that look like? Write your version below:

2. I use the metaphor of a body to refer to the intellectual structure. I almost used the metaphor of a building. Write the content of the second paragraph here, but use the metaphor of a building, such as a skyscraper or a house. Think of the highest and the lowest stuff involved with such edifices.

3. Find statements in the textbook that back up what is argued in the second and third paragraphs. List those statements here.

4. This section ends by announcing some examples. Based on what you've learned (if not come to believe) in this course, write the next two to three paragraphs that seem to satisfy the expectations that examples will be given.

5. In what ways does this topic reflect your experience of college so far?

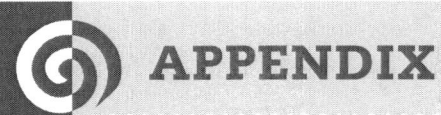
Grammatical Terms Necessary for PRE Analysis

GRAMMATICAL TERMS TO KNOW: Understand the following words in terms of their function in a sentence and their relationship to the other parts of a sentence.

Subject

1. There are two ways to use this word:

   a. The term can refer to the grammatical subject.

   b. The term can refer to the topic of the sentence or passage.

      i. Whenever I ask, "What is the subject in this sentence?" I am referring the first definition, to the grammatical subject.

      ii. When I am referring to the second definition, I will ask, "What is the topic of the sentence, or what is it about?"

2. These are the traits of the subject in terms of its identity and function:

   a. A subject is always a noun.

   b. It comes before the verb.

   c. It can be an actor, a receiver, or described.

   d. Sometimes the subject can be a nominalization, and then we have to be careful about its use.

Verb

1. Verbs usually convey action, **and action can be conveyed in the active or the passive voice**.

2. verbs can also convey a state of being.

   a. *Be* verbs (*is, were, was, are*): these are like **equal signs, used to describe things**.

      i. For example: History is bunk.

      ii. Scoundrels are sociable.

   b. *Has, had*: these verbs are like equal signs; they convey no action.

      i. He had to go to work.

      ii. He has to be on time.

3. Some verbs contain vague action: *led*, *hold*, etc.

4. NOTE: Verb VOICE has nothing to do with time markers.

   a. **That is, "passive voice" DOES NOT refer to "past tense."**

Noun

1. A noun is a person, place, or thing.

2. A nominalization is a noun derived from a verb or adjective.

3. Grammatical subjects have to be nouns.

Verb Voice

Voice refers to the **relationship** between the subject and its verb.

NOTE: Verb voices does NOT refer to verb tense, like past or present.

1. **Active voice** means that the subject is **performing the action** of the verb.

   a. The subject is actively doing something.

   b. Readers prefer subjects to be performing the action of the verb, instead of receiving the action of the verb.

   c. So, readers expect active-voice verbs.

   d. Here is a simple sentence that has an active-voice verb:

      i. The student wrote the paper.

      ii. Other examples: The student is writing the paper; the student was writing the paper; the student had written the paper.

2. **Passive voice** means the subject is **receiving the action** of the verb.

   a. The subject is a passive character in relation to the action of the sentence.

   b. Readers can understand the proper use of passive voice.

   c. Here is a simple sentence that uses passive voice:

      i. The paper was written by the student.

      ii. Notice that passive voice almost always has to use some form of *is* in its verb form.

      iii. Other examples: The paper was written by the student; the paper will be written by the student; the paper had been written by the student.

3. Sometimes a *be* verb isn't used in passive voice, but you can still identify whether the voice of the verb is active or passive by **identifying the relation of the subject to the verb.**

   a. Ask: Is the subject performing the action of the verb? If so, the verb is active voice.

   b. Ask: Is the subject receiving the action of the verb? If so, the verb is passive voice.

4. Readers expect active-voice verbs but will accept passive-voice verbs if they can see why they were used.

5. However, dense, **difficult writing** is often caused by an **overuse of passive-voice verbs AND the overuse of nominalizations in the subject position**.

Clause

1. There are dependent and independent clauses.

2. Any clause has a subject and verb in it.

3. But some clauses are constructed so that you can't put a period after the complete clause.

   a. For example, you can't put a period after this clause:

   b. When the teacher graded the paper

      i. This is an incomplete thought.

      ii. The word *when* implies that more will be said after the first subject and verb.

      iii. We have here a dependent clause, created by the subordinate conjunction *when*.

4. We have some choices:
   a. Make the dependent clause an independent one.
      i. We do this by dropping *when*.
      ii. The teacher graded the paper.
   b. Or, add an independent clause:
      i. When the teacher handed back the papers, the students groaned.
5. A simple sentence is a single independent clause.
   a. But many sentences consist of combinations of independent and dependent clauses.
   b. They may also consist of other units of words, but that is all we will look at right now.

Prepositions

1. These are little words that introduce nouns:
   a. **Of** the people, **by** the people, **for** the people
   b. **Over** the river, and **through** the woods, **to** grandmother's house we go

Coordination

The basis of elegant style is simple. It is REPETITION of an element in a BALANCED way.

1. You can repeat a word or words:
   a. **When we** work hard, **when we** play hard, **when we** sleep hard, we live well.
   b. After he came home, he **worked**, she **worked**, they **worked**.
2. You can repeat a grammatical term, such as a preposition:
   a. **of** the people, **by** the people, **for** the people
3. You can repeat phrasings:
   a. We will work for play, and we will play for work, but we will not work for work's sake.
4. Coordinating sentences is pretty easy, once you see it is a matter of repeating some element in the sentence.

5. You should do this with important material, showing relationships among diverse elements of the issue.

6. Coordination is good to use at dramatic moments in your essay, especially in the opening or closing.

Remember

1. These terms and concepts deal with the **relationships** of words within a sentence.

2. These terms help you describe how parts of a sentence function with other parts of a sentence.

   a. For instance, is the subject receiving the action of the verb?

   b. Or is the subject performing the action of the verb?

   c. Or is the verb an equal sign, so the subject is getting described by the words that follow the *is* verb?

3. These concepts don't really look at the grammar of the sentence.

4. These terms help you describe how a sentence observes or violates the reader's expectations.

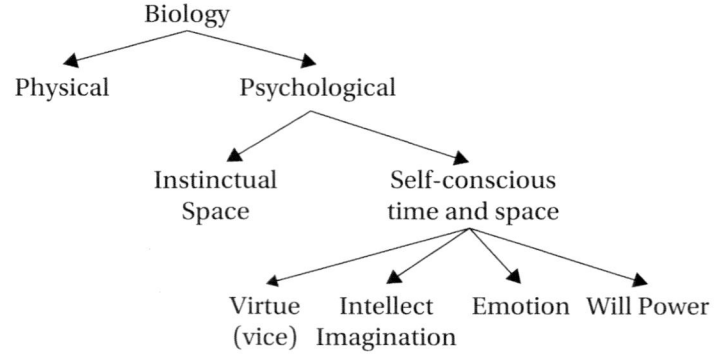

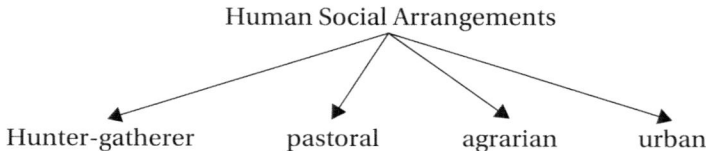

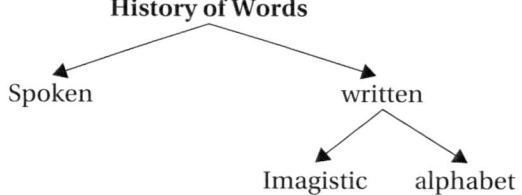

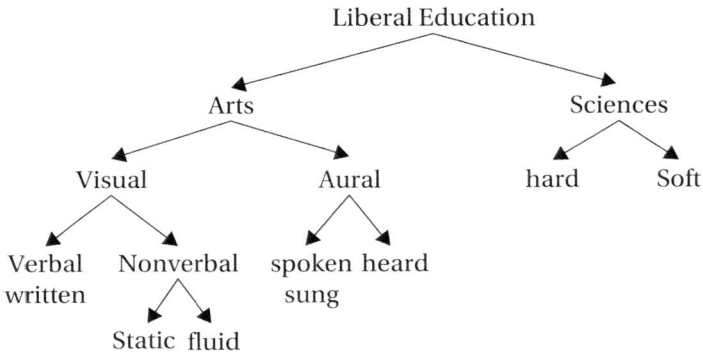

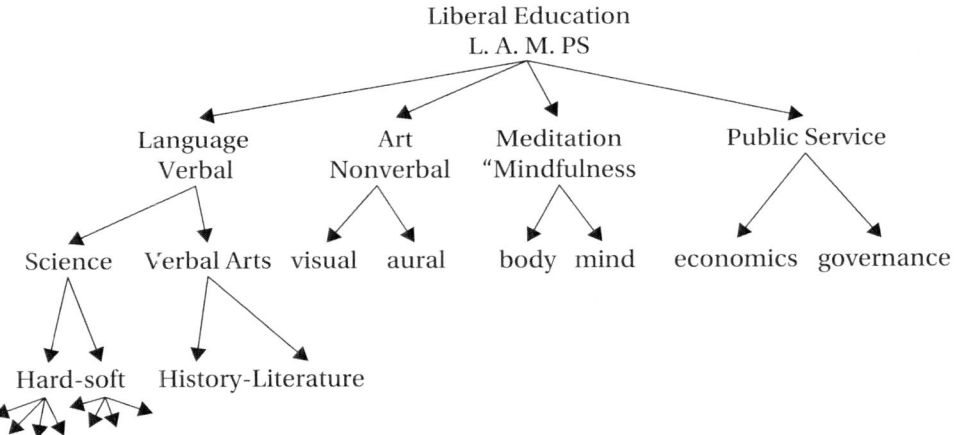

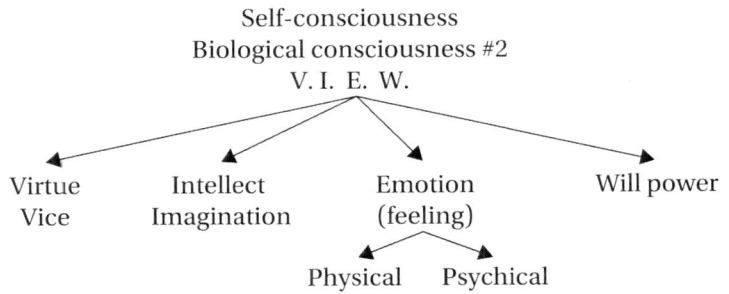

Index

A

Abstract
  definition, 61
  revision of, 81, 83
Academic prose sentence
  reading, 142–143
  revising, 143–145
Academic readers, 100
  comparison with civilian readers, 56
  expectations, 101
    of paragraphs (abbreviated form), 101
    of paragraphs (long form), 101–103
    of sentence structure, 141
    of sentence-structure variables, 106
    of sentences (abbreviated form),
      100–101
    of sentences (long form), 101–103
Academic text passages
  issue of understanding, 196
  reading method for, 60–65
Academic writers, sources of bad writing by,
    104–105
Active-voice verb (AVV), 50, 62, 65
  definition, 264
  to passive-voice verb, 81, 83, 157
Adult-level understanding, 4, 8, 9, 21, 153,
    243–244, 248, 249
  enlightened, 5, 9
  inadequate, 6
Adult realism, 242–244
Annotated bibliography, 203–205, 229
Anthology, 217
APA (American Psychological Association)
    format, 216, 227–228
Arts & Humanities Research Council, 64

Assumptions, 76
  bring into college
    faculties, 3–4
    students, 2–3, 8–10
  about inexperienced writers, 40–41
  rewriting in response to revision analysis,
    49–50
Attitudes
  of experienced readers, 59
  of inexperienced writers, 40–41
  play, in writing process, 42–43
  rewriting in response to revision analysis, 49
  work, in writing process, 42, 44–45
  toward writing process, 65–68
Audience appeal, 48–49
Avatar, 9–10

B

Berthoff, Anne, 75
Bible, 197, 198–199, 204–205, 230
Bibliography, 216–221
  annotated, 203–205
  anthologies, conventions to apply,
    218–219
  for book by an editor, 217
  for book other than first edition, 218
  for book with a translator, 218
  for book with two/three authors, 217
  correcting formats of, 229–230
  periodical, 219–221
  search, 209, 211
  for single-author book, 216
  for two/more books by same author, 218
  for work from anthology, 217
Bizzell, Patricia, 75